The Covenant of God with Abraham Opened and Other Works
by William Carter
with chapters by C. Matthew McMahon

Copyright Information

The Covenant of God with Abraham Opened and Other Works, by William Carter, with chapters by C. Matthew McMahon
Edited by Therese B. McMahon

Copyright ©2025 by Puritan Publications and A Puritan's Mind®

Some language and grammar have been updated from original manuscripts. Any change in wording or punctuation has not changed the intent or meaning of the original author(s) and has been made to aid the modern reader with gently updated language.

Published by Puritan Publications
A Ministry of A Puritan's Mind® in Crossville, TN.
www.apuritansmind.com
www.puritanpublications.com
www.gracechapeltn.com
www.reformedsynod.com

All rights reserved. No part of this publication may be reproduced, stored in a retrieval system or transmitted in any form by any means, electronic, mechanical, photocopy, recording or otherwise, without the prior permission of the publisher, except as provided by USA copyright law.

This Print Edition, 2025
Electronic Edition, 2025

Manufactured in the United States of America

ISBN: 978-1-62663-511-1
eISBN: 978-1-62663-510-4

Table of Contents

Meet William Carter 4

William Carter's View of Covenant 9

The Covenant of God with Abraham Opened...................15

Sufficiency and Superiority 109

A Short Discourse 122

Light in Darkness..171

Israel's Peace with God 192

Other Works Published by Westminster Divines at Puritan Publications..217

Meet William Carter
By C. Matthew McMahon, Ph.D., Th.D.

William Carter (1605–1658) was the kind of man who, if handed a plow, would have carved furrows straight through rocky soil and thorny fields, driven by a singular devotion to his Maker and a burning compassion for the souls of his fellow man. His life was a picture of learning, preaching, and unrelenting labor in the service of God. Though his years were few, his impact was substantial, leaving a legacy of theological insight and pastoral dedication that continues to beckon the thoughtful reader.

A Scholar of Great Depth

Born in 1605, Carter honed his sharp intellect at Cambridge, where he laid the groundwork for a career marked by rigorous study and theological depth. He wasn't one to waste his days in idle speculations; rather, he pressed every moment into the service of gaining wisdom, which he would later wield like a sharp-edged tool in his ministry. This scholarly rigor, combined with a heartfelt piety to Christ, caught the eye of his contemporaries and earned him a seat among the Assembly of Divines at Westminster—a distinction not lightly bestowed, especially on a man so young.

The Assembly was no mere gathering of idle talkers. It was a convergence of some of the sharpest theological minds of the age, charged with the task of crafting a doctrinal foundation for the reformation of the Church of

England, Ireland and Scotland. In their midst, Carter stood, not as a passive observer, but as an *active* participant. He debated earnestly on matters like the divine institution of church offices, advocating alongside other notable Independents for a robust vision of pastoral and teaching ministry. His arguments, though tempered by the need for consensus, reflected a mind deeply engaged with the Scriptures and committed to their practical application.

A Minister of Tireless Devotion

Carter's life was not confined to the intellectual halls of Cambridge or the deliberative chambers of the Westminster Assembly. His sincere calling was to the pulpit and the people. London, a bustling city of commerce and chaos, became his vineyard, and he labored in it with relentless zeal. His preaching, marked by both clarity and conviction, drew large congregations eager to hear the Word of God rightly divided.

He preached twice each Sunday to eager throngs and held additional lectures during the week. These were not casual talks tossed together in a flurry of deadlines, but the outpouring of a man whose heart burned for the spiritual welfare of his hearers. Carter's ministry was not a detached or clinical exercise; it was deeply personal. His affection for his congregation was evident, as Paul wrote to the Thessalonians: "We were willing to have imparted unto you, not the gospel of God only, but also our own souls, because ye were dear unto us," (1 Thessalonians 2:8).

His heart ached for the careless and the unconverted. He mourned their hardness of heart in private and longed to see the transforming work of grace in their lives. Carter understood well the stakes of his work, the eternal destiny of souls. His preaching and teaching were aimed squarely at this end, and he would not spare himself in the effort.

Works of Enduring Value

Though Carter's voice no longer thunders from the pulpit, his writings remain, offering a glimpse into the mind and heart of this faithful servant. His published works, including "Israels Peace with God" (1642), "Light in Darkness" (1648), and "The Covenant of God with Abraham Opened" (1654), reflect his rich theological understanding and his pastoral concerns.

In *Light in Darkness*, preached before the House of Commons during a solemn fast, Carter draws from Psalm 65:5: "By terrible things in righteousness wilt thou answer us, O God of our salvation." Here, he demonstrates his gift for applying Scripture to the pressing concerns of the day, addressing not only personal piety but also the broader social and political realities of his time. His sermons reveal a preacher who understood the weight of his calling and the importance of addressing both the hearts and minds of his audience.

Carter's treatment of the covenant in *The Covenant of God with Abraham Opened* reflects a deep appreciation for the continuity of God's redemptive work across history. He shows how God's promises to Abraham find their ultimate fulfillment in Christ and extend to all who are heirs of the promise through faith. This work underscores Carter's commitment to grounding theological truth in the bedrock of Scripture, offering timeless insights into the nature of God's grace and faithfulness.

A Life Poured Out

Carter's labors were not without cost. His ceaseless dedication to preaching, teaching, and pastoral care took its toll. By the time he fell asleep in the Lord in 1658, at just 53 years of age, his body bore the marks of a life spent in service to others. Yet, there was no bitterness in his sacrifice, no begrudging of the years given to God's work. He had learned, as Paul did, to count all things but loss for the excellency of knowing Christ and making Him known.

In his ministry, Carter embodied the words of 1 Peter 4:10-11: "As every man hath received the gift, even so minister the same one to another, as good stewards of the manifold grace of God. If any man speak, let him speak as the oracles of God; if any man minister, let him do it as of the ability which God giveth." His life was a stewardship, and he spent it well, leaving behind not wealth or fame, but a legacy of faithfulness and truth.

A Legacy Worth Remembering

The life and work of William Carter offer a lasting example for ministers and laypeople alike. His commitment to the Scriptures, his tireless efforts in the vineyard of the Lord, and his heartfelt compassion for the lost stand as a testament to the power of a life fully surrendered to God. He reminds us that the Christian life is not one of ease but of labor—a labor infused with joy and hope because it is grounded in the finished work of Christ.

Carter's writings continue to bear witness to the truths he held dear: the sufficiency of Scripture, the centrality of Christ, and the necessity of diligent effort in the pursuit of godliness. His legacy, though forged in a different time and place, speaks clearly to the challenges and opportunities of our own day. For those who will heed his example, there is much to learn from this faithful servant of God, who in his short life accomplished much for the glory of his Savior and the good of His Church.

William Carter's View of Covenant
By C. Matthew McMahon, Ph.D., Th.D.

It is no small task to bring clarity and correction to a subject as sacred and enduring as the covenant of God with His people. Yet, in the work before us, William Carter undertakes this labor with both the careful precision of a minister suited to exposition and exegesis, and the fervent passion of a divine utterly committed to the truth. This work is a defense of Reformed orthodoxy and a demonstration of the abiding importance of God's covenantal dealings with His Church, particularly as it pertains to the application of the covenant sign and the status of believers' children within that sacred agreement. Its foundation rests upon the Scriptures, most prominently Genesis 17, which establishes God's covenant with Abraham and his seed, and it unfolds with the deliberate aim of fortifying the Church against the errors that have crept in regarding these doctrines.

At the heart of this treatise is a simple yet vital premise: God has, from the beginning, worked *through covenants* to reveal Himself, to save a people unto Himself, and to bring His blessings to those whom He has chosen. The covenant established with Abraham, marked by the seal of circumcision, is shown to be a continuation of God's eternal plan, now fulfilled in Christ and extended to the New Testament Church through baptism. The author takes great care to demonstrate that this covenant, which was once sealed by the blood of circumcision, is now confirmed by the waters of baptism. It is, as he rightly argues, a single covenant of grace under two administrations, the latter being a fuller revelation of God's mercy and love in Christ Jesus.

The first point addressed with precision is the promise God made to Abraham: "I will establish my covenant between me and thee and thy seed after thee in their generations for an everlasting covenant, to be a God unto thee, and to thy seed after thee," (Genesis 17:7). This foundational Scripture is central to Carter's argument, showing that the covenant of grace is not limited to Abraham alone but extends to his spiritual seed across all generations, fulfilled in the Seed, Jesus Christ mystically considered. The promise is not merely individualistic; it is familial and generational, encompassing the children of believers as integral participants in the covenant. The *application* of the covenant seal to infants is therefore not an innovation but a continuation of what God Himself has instituted.

Carter anticipates objections with clarity and addresses them with the weight of Scriptural evidence and logical reasoning. One such objection centers on the supposed silence of the New Testament regarding the baptism of infants. To this, the author points to Acts 2:38–39, where Peter declares, "Repent, and be baptized every one of you in the name of Jesus Christ for the remission of sins, and ye shall receive the gift of the Holy Ghost. For the promise is unto you, and to your children, and to all that are afar off, even as many as the Lord our God shall call." This text, he argues, affirms the continuity of the covenantal promise and its application to believers and their offspring. The inclusion of children within the covenant is not a matter of speculation but a truth rooted in God's unchanging Word.

Moreover, he does not shy away from addressing the errors of those who, like the Baptists, deny the covenantal inclusion of infants. He meticulously dismantles their arguments, showing that to withhold the covenant seal from children is to *break* Abraham's covenant (Christ's covenant), for the promise is clear: "And ye shall circumcise the flesh of your foreskin; and it shall be a token of the covenant betwixt me and you," (Genesis 17:11). To exclude children from the covenant sign is to undermine the promise itself, which explicitly includes them. His argument is neither harsh nor dismissive but firm and unwavering, as he seeks to preserve the truth of God's covenant against misinterpretation.

In a similar vein, the author turns his attention to the errors of Roman Catholicism, particularly their misunderstanding of the nature of God's covenant and the sufficiency of Christ's work. While the Catholics have erred in exalting human tradition above Scripture, Carter demonstrates that the covenant of grace is grounded solely in God's promise and Christ's *finished* work. The blessings of the covenant are not dispensed solely by the authority of the Church but by the Spirit of God through faith in Christ. Baptism, as the seal of the covenant, is a sign of God's faithfulness, not a means of human merit, or the infusion of a losable kind of grace as the Papists maintain.

The work also explores the practical implications of covenant theology for the life of the Church and the family. One of the most compelling aspects of the argument is the responsibility of parents to raise their children in the fear and admonition of the Lord. The author cites Genesis 18:19, where God commends Abraham, saying, "For I know him, that he will command his children and his household after him, and they shall keep the way of the LORD, to do justice and judgment." This text highlights the necessity of family instruction and discipleship, which Carter emphasizes as a means of advancing God's kingdom. Parents are not merely to hope for their children's salvation but to actively engage in their spiritual formation, trusting that God's promise to bless families will be fulfilled.

Carter also addresses the nature of the Church as a visible body, composed of both believers *and* their children. He argues that the inclusion of children within the covenant and the Church is not a matter of human tradition but divine ordinance. This inclusion, he asserts, reflects the gracious character of God, who delights to bring whole households into His kingdom. As Joshua declared, "As for me and my house, we will serve the LORD," (Joshua 24:15), so too must every believing family submit their children to the covenant and its blessings.

While the work is deeply theological, it is also pastoral. Carter does not merely refute error; he calls the reader to faithfulness and obedience. He exhorts believers to *walk* in the steps of Abraham, teaching their families, living uprightly, and maintaining a close and vibrant relationship with God. The blessings of the covenant are not automatic;

they are realized *through* faith and perseverance. As the Apostle Paul writes, "Be ye followers of them who through faith and patience inherit the promises," (Hebrews 6:12). This call to perseverance is a reminder that covenant blessings are inseparably linked to covenant faithfulness.

The concluding chapters of the work emphasize the ultimate triumph of Christ's kingdom. Drawing from passages such as Isaiah 60 and Revelation 21, Carter envisions a time when the kingdom of God will fill the earth, and the nations will submit to Christ's rule. This *eschatological* hope is not merely an abstract concept but a reality grounded in the promises of Scripture. The kingdom will grow, not through coercion or political power, but through the faithful proclamation of the Gospel and the multiplication of Abraham's seed. The Church's mission, therefore, is to labor in the power of the Spirit to make disciples, trusting that God will fulfill His promise to bless all nations through Christ.

This work is a treasure for the Church, not only as a defense of covenant theology but as a guide for faithful living. It refutes errors that undermine the promises of God and calls believers to embrace their covenantal responsibilities with joy and gratitude. By rooting its arguments in Scripture and expounding them with clarity and conviction, the author provides a robust foundation for understanding God's covenantal dealings with His people. It is a command to faithfulness, a light of truth in a world of error, and a testimony to the unchanging faithfulness of God, who declares, "I will be their God, and they shall be my people," (Jeremiah 31:33). Through this work, the Church is reminded of the glorious privilege of being in covenant with the Almighty and the weighty responsibility of living as His covenant people.

In Christ's grace and mercy,
C. Matthew McMahon, Ph.D., Th.D.
From My study, February, 2025
"...search the Scriptures..." (John 5:39).
www.apuritansmind.com
www.puritanpublications.com
www.gracechapeltn.com
www.reformedsynod.com

The Covenant of God with Abraham Opened

To the Reader

What I intended to present on the subject of infant baptism, I have condensed into as small a space as possible. For this reason, I have *deliberately* avoided answering every objection raised by those who disagree with me. Neither have I listed all, or even many, arguments to prove the position I assert here. Instead, I have focused on what I believe to be the most important argument: the explicit command of God to Abraham's descendants in Genesis 17:9 to observe the token of His covenant throughout their generations. Baptism is now the token and seal of this covenant, as circumcision was, and the application of it to infants is part of that token.

The dissatisfaction many experience in this matter, as in other cases, often stems from a lack of effort in searching out the truth. Therefore, I did not wish to burden my reader with an overly lengthy volume. Solomon says we must seek wisdom as we would seek silver and search for it as we would for hidden treasures (Proverbs 2:4). In such a pursuit, we should not stop at merely uncovering minor veins of silver but should follow them to discover the larger body of the mine. Scripture provides many hints of this truth scattered throughout, but the root of the matter lies in God's covenant with Abraham, and it is to this covenant that I have primarily confined my discussion.

The reason I have written at this length is the vast scope of this covenant, as it serves as a summary of the entire gospel of the kingdom. In explaining it, I could not avoid addressing various aspects of Christ's kingdom. Regarding the Sabbath, I have also been compelled to expand somewhat, as I find it to be a parallel case to infant baptism. In pursuing my text, I have paused to explain the third and fourth chapters of the Epistle to the Hebrews, briefly summarizing some key points I treated more extensively in past years on the subject of the Sabbath.

Additionally, I could not avoid digressing into the doctrine of *the Law*. This was necessary to defend and encourage the study of the Old Testament as foundational for a proper understanding of the Sabbath, as well as other ordinances of worship, including infant baptism. May the Holy Spirit, who is the Comforter of God's people, lead us into all truth and guide our feet into the way of peace.

This is the prayer of your servant in the gospel,
WILLIAM CARTER

The Covenant of God with Abraham Opened

Hebrews 6:13-18, "For when God made promise to Abraham, because he could swear by no greater, he sware by himself, saying, Surely, blessing I will bless thee, and multiplying I will multiply thee. And so, after he had patiently endured, he obtained the promise. For men verily swear by the greater: and an oath for confirmation is to them an end of all strife. Wherein God, willing more abundantly to show unto the heirs of promise the immutability of his counsel, confirmed it by an oath: that by two immutable things, in which it was impossible for God to lie, we might have a strong consolation, who have fled for refuge to lay hold upon the hope set before us."

In explaining this passage, it is essential to first consider the Apostle's purpose throughout this epistle for greater clarity. He addresses this epistle to *believing* Hebrews, or at least to those who *profess* faith in Christ. This is evident from his reference to them as "holy brethren, partakers of the heavenly calling," and his declaration that Christ was their Apostle and High Priest (Hebrews 3:1). They had been taught "the doctrine of Christ" (Hebrews 5-6) and were commended for their "labor of love" in ministering to the saints (Hebrews 6). They are assumed to be *members* of a Christian church (Hebrews 13:7, 17).

However, many of these believers were abandoning the ordinances of New Testament worship and forsaking their holy profession, of which Christ is the Apostle and High Priest. They were reverting to Moses, as seen in this epistle and others, especially Galatians. The Apostle's primary aim in this letter is to prevent and remedy this apostasy. This is evident because his many arguments consistently conclude with exhortations to hold fast to their faith and liberty.

For instance, after presenting an argument in Hebrews 4:14, he concludes, "Having therefore such an High Priest, Jesus the Son of God, who is entered into the heavens, let us hold fast our profession." Again, in verse 16, he encourages, "Let us come with boldness unto the throne of grace," with the term "boldness" (Greek: *parrhesia*) also translated as "liberty". This contrasts with the bondage of Jewish worship, where access to the mercy seat was restricted, keeping worshippers outside the veil (Hebrews 9:8).

In chapters 7 through 9, the Apostle argues that with Christ's coming, there was a necessary change in the priesthood and the law governing worship. After completing this argument, he concludes in Hebrews 10:19, "Having therefore, brethren, boldness to enter into the holiest by the blood of Jesus, and having an High Priest over the house of God, let us draw near with a true heart in full assurance of faith." He also urges, "Let us hold fast the profession of our faith without wavering, not forsaking the assembling of ourselves together, as the manner of some is," (Hebrews 10:23–25). Further, in verse 35, he warns, "Cast not away therefore your confidence," (*parrhesia*).

The bondage of the Jews primarily involved the ordinances and forms of Old Testament worship (Galatians 4:9). While their personal standing by faith was the same as ours, being under the covenant of grace and justified by faith, the restrictions of their worship practices contrasted sharply with the liberty of New Testament worship. The Apostle exhorts believers not to abandon the worship of the New Testament in favor of the old.

In Hebrews 12:15–16, he warns believers not to "sell their birthright." The birthright of believers refers to their *privileges* in the gospel's church and worship, which they were at risk of forfeiting. This again points to the contrast between the Old and New Testaments in the latter part of that chapter.

Finally, in Hebrews 4:9, the Apostle declares, "There remaineth therefore the keeping of a Sabbath for the people of God." This conclusion arises from his argument beginning in Hebrews 3:7, which quotes Psalm 95. Here, New Testament believers are prophetically exhorted: "O come, let us worship and bow down: let us kneel before the Lord our maker. For he is our God; and we are the people of his pasture, and the sheep of his hand. Today, if ye will hear his voice, harden not your heart," (Psalm 95:6–8).

Our Savior, Jesus Christ, declares, "I am the good Shepherd, and my sheep will hear my voice," (John 10:14, 27). Thus, believers are called to worship because it is Christ, the great Shepherd of our souls, who invites us. We are warned not to harden our hearts as the Israelites did in the wilderness, where He was also their Shepherd, called "the Shepherd of Israel", (Psalm 80:1). As Psalm 77:20 declares, "Thou leddest thy people like a flock by the hand of Moses and Aaron."

As our Shepherd, Christ performs two primary acts: He feeds us and gives us rest. "Tell me, O thou whom my soul loveth, where thou feedest, where thou makest thy flock to rest at noon," (Song of Solomon 1:7). Because He provides rest, the Apostle warns that we must not provoke Him to swear in His wrath as He did against those in the wilderness, that they would not enter His rest.

The Apostle, using Psalm 95, seeks to persuade believers of the necessity of Gospel worship and, within that context, demonstrates the continuation of the Christian Sabbath. In chapters three and four of Hebrews, he establishes the connection between the two, showing that those who accept one cannot deny the other. Having laid out his arguments, he concludes in Hebrews 4:9, "There remaineth therefore the keeping of a Sabbath for the people of God." He does not say simply that a Sabbath remains, but rather that a *Sabbatism* (Greek: σαββατισμός) remains—a "celebration of a Sabbath" for God's people. This term encompasses not only the Sabbath itself but also its proper observance in God's house *through instituted worship*. Thus, the Apostle declares that "the celebration of a Sabbath remains for the people of God," aiming to counteract their abandonment of both the Christian Sabbath and Gospel worship.

Understanding the Apostle's goal in this epistle is crucial to grasping the broader argument. It is equally important to examine the methods he employs to persuade his readers. First, he highlights that while the Old Testament ordinances were delivered by angels and through Moses (Galatians 3:19, Hebrews 2:2, Acts 7:53), the ordinances of the New Testament come directly from Christ. In the first two chapters of Hebrews, the Apostle emphasizes Christ's superiority over angels, and in the third chapter, he exalts Christ above Moses. He writes, "Consider the Apostle and High Priest of our profession, Christ Jesus, who was faithful to him that appointed him, as Moses also was faithful in all his house," (Hebrews 3:1–2). Christ is presented as the builder of the house, the Creator of the world, and God Himself (Hebrews 3:4). Moses, by contrast, is merely a stone in the building, a servant in the house, while Christ is the Son and rightful *owner*.

Having laid this foundation, the Apostle addresses his main subject. Referring to the house of Christ, he states in Hebrews 3:6, "Whose house are we, if we hold fast the confidence and the rejoicing of the hope firm unto the end." This "confidence" (again, *parrhesia* in Greek, also translated as "liberty") refers to their steadfast adherence to the ordinances and privileges of Gospel worship. The Jewish ordinances represented bondage, as the law "made nothing perfect" (Hebrews 7:19), but the Gospel introduced a better hope by which believers can draw near to God. Thus, their perseverance in Gospel worship is described as holding fast both liberty and hope.

The Apostle further connects this theme to the house of God as a place of rest, citing Isaiah 66:1, "Where is the house that ye build unto me? and where is the place of my rest?" and Psalm 132:8, 14, "Arise, O Lord, into thy rest; thou, and the ark of thy strength... This is my rest forever: here will I dwell; for I have desired it." He exhorts his readers not to reject Christ's offer of rest in His house, drawing upon the words of David in Psalm 95. Here, the Apostle finds a ready-made exhortation: "Wherefore (as the Holy Ghost saith) Today if ye will hear his voice, harden not your hearts, as in the provocation, in the day of temptation in the wilderness: when your fathers tempted me, proved me, and saw my works forty years. Wherefore I was grieved with that generation, and said, They do always err in their heart; and they have not known my ways. So I sware in my wrath, They shall not enter into my rest," (Hebrews 3:7–11).

The Apostle presses believers to heed Christ's voice because He is their Shepherd, and they are "the people of his pasture, and the sheep of his hand," (Psalm 95:7). He varies the title, calling Christ the "Apostle and High Priest of our profession," yet speaks of the *same* relationship. What Christ accomplishes as the Apostle and High Priest in His house, He also does as the great Shepherd of souls. This is seen in Psalm 23, where David describes the blessings of dwelling in the Lord's house, concluding, "I will dwell in the house of the Lord forever," (Psalm 23:6). He attributes this to Christ's role as Shepherd, "The Lord is my shepherd; I shall not want. He maketh me to lie down in green pastures, he leadeth me beside the still waters," (Psalm 23:1–2).

As Shepherd, Christ provides two essential blessings: nourishment and rest. "He maketh me to lie down in green pastures," (Psalm 23:2), feeding His flock and giving them rest even "in the presence of [*their*] enemies" (Psalm 23:5). These blessings are found in Christ Himself—He is both our Bread of Life and our Rest. He has also prepared a house of rest, His Church, where He feeds His people and grants them rest "at noon" (Song of Solomon 1:7). Within this house, He has appointed a day of rest to be celebrated through worship.

Unlike wild beasts that fend for themselves, Christ's sheep live under His guidance. They are called "the sheep of his hand," (Psalm 95:7), signifying His governance, as seen in Psalm 77:20: "Thou leddest thy people like a flock by the hand of Moses and Aaron." His sheep recognize His voice and gather as His flock in His house, worshipping on the day He has appointed. The Psalmist exhorts, "O come, let us worship and bow down: let us kneel before the Lord our maker... Today if ye will hear his voice," (Psalm 95:6–7).

All this Christ accomplishes as Shepherd and as the Apostle and High Priest of our profession. As such, He faithfully appoints His house and its ordinances, just as He was faithful to the One who appointed Him (Hebrews 3:2). Moreover, He is "Lord also of the Sabbath," (Matthew 12:8), having sanctified the day for His service. Each Sabbath is as though we hear His voice inviting us to rest with Him in His house. This is why the Psalmist depicts God's people exhorting one another, saying, "O come, let us worship... Today if ye will hear his voice." Since the other six days are designated for labor (Exodus 20:9), it is on this holy day that the saints are called to worship.

I have chosen to dwell at length on this topic because it will be helpful in understanding God's covenant with Abraham, as will soon be evident. Additionally, these two chapters—Hebrews 3 and 4—provide a clear foundation for the Christian Sabbath, which I will later connect to the subject of infant baptism, the primary focus of this discourse. For this reason, I will continue examining these chapters before addressing my primary text, showing from the Apostle's words that the phrase, "Today if ye will hear his voice," in Psalm 95, refers to the Christian Sabbath. This can be demonstrated *as follows:*

First, it is clear that the phrase refers to a day of rest, as seen in Hebrews 4:7–8: "He limiteth a certain day, saying in David, Today, after so long a time, as it is said, Today if ye will hear his voice, harden not your hearts. For if Joshua had given them rest, then would he not afterward have spoken of another day." This argument shows that it must refer to a day of rest, or the Apostle's reasoning would lack coherence. Even if Joshua had provided them with the rest mentioned, it would not negate the mention of another day. Thus, the reference to another day must concern rest.

Second, the rest in question is one concerning which God can, and sometimes does, swear in His wrath that His people, who are His house and the sheep of His pasture, will not enter it. This cannot apply merely to the rest believers enjoy through personal faith, but it can relate to the *comfort* of His ordinances and the Sabbath. This connection will become clearer when we examine God's promise to Abraham.

Third, the Apostle's reasoning makes it evident that this rest refers to the Sabbath day. He demonstrates that it is a distinct day of rest, separate from those previously observed in the church. It stands in contrast to the seventh-day Sabbath because David speaks of it as a rest to be entered into long after the seventh-day rest had been observed from the beginning of the world. As the Apostle writes, "He spake in a certain place of the seventh day on this wise, And God did rest the seventh day from all his works. And in this place again, If they shall enter into my rest," (Hebrews 4:4–5). This implies a promise that some will enter into this rest while others will not. Since David speaks of a rest to come, and since he limits a certain day, saying "Today," the Apostle concludes, "There remaineth therefore a rest to the people of God," referring to a Sabbath distinct from the seventh-day Sabbath. By this reasoning, the Apostle demonstrates that "Today if ye will hear his voice," does not merely refer to a believer's personal rest by faith—which is enjoyed every day and has been since the beginning of the world—but to a new Sabbath rest established under the New Testament.

Fourth, this rest is connected to the worship of God in His house. The Apostle concludes in Hebrews 4:9, "There remaineth therefore a Sabbatism [σαββατισμός], the celebration of a Sabbath for the people of God." This word combines the concepts of Sabbath *and* worship. This connection is further supported by the coherence of Psalm 95, which declares, "O come, let us worship and bow down: let us kneel before the Lord our maker. For he is our God; and we are the people of his pasture, and the sheep of his hand. Today if ye will hear his voice, harden not your hearts," (Psalm 95:6–8). Similarly, the Apostle applies this, saying, "His house are we; wherefore, as the Holy Ghost saith, Today if ye will hear his voice," (Hebrews 3:6–7). Thus, the "voice" refers to Christ calling His people to worship and rest with Him in His house on this day.

Fifth, the Apostle identifies this rest with Christ's cessation from His works and His entering into rest, just as the seventh-day Sabbath was connected to God's cessation from His works after creation. Hebrews 4:10 states, "For he that is entered into his rest, he also hath ceased from his own works, as God did from his." This rest is tied to Christ, as is evident from the Apostle's subsequent argument: "Seeing then that we have a great high priest, that is passed into the heavens, Jesus the Son of God, let us hold fast our profession," (Hebrews 4:14). This statement connects directly to Christ's entering into His rest, as His passing into the heavens is a necessary component of that rest.

To clarify this connection further, it is necessary to adjust the translation of Hebrews 4:10 slightly. The words "his own" should not apply to the first clause, as though referring to a believer ceasing from sin, but rather to the latter clause: "He also hath ceased from his works, as God did from his own works." This aligns with the Greek text (καθάπερ ἀπὸ τῶν ἰδίων ὁ Θεός), indicating that Christ ceased from His works *just as* God ceased from His after creation.

The Apostle further strengthens this argument by applying Psalm 95 to Christ. In the Psalm, the Lord is described as "our maker," whose voice we are called to hear and before whom we are to bow in worship. The Apostle applies this directly to Christ, the builder of the house and all things, who is God (Hebrews 3:4). He concludes, "His house are we; wherefore, Today if ye will hear his voice, harden not your hearts," (Hebrews 3:6–7). Thus, the voice to which believers are called to listen is that of Christ, our maker and Lord.

Finally, the Apostle connects this rest to Christ's entering into His rest, making it clear that this Sabbath day of worship is grounded in Christ's completed work and rest, just as the seventh-day Sabbath was grounded in God's rest after creation.

Thirdly, the rest referred to in this passage cannot signify merely ceasing from sin. This is because it is described as a ceasing akin to God's ceasing from His works—a rest in which God found satisfaction in what He had accomplished. God's rest was not merely a negative act of refraining from labor but a positive enjoyment of what He had done. As Exodus 31:17 states, "He rested the seventh day, and was refreshed." When God looked upon His work, He declared it to be "very good" (Genesis 1:31). In contrast, one who ceases from sin views it as evil and finds no satisfaction in it.

Fourthly, the Apostle's argument in Hebrews 4:10 demonstrates that this rest signifies another Sabbath or day of rest remaining for God's people. This rest is distinct from that which had existed from the beginning of the world (Hebrews 4:3) or in the time of Joshua (Hebrews 4:8). Ceasing from sin or resting in Christ by faith does not establish such a new Sabbath rest.

Fifthly, consider what Christ says of Himself: "The Son of man is Lord also of the Sabbath," (Mark 2:28, Luke 6:5). Christ is Lord of heaven and earth, of His house, and of His worship. "There are diversities of administrations, but the same Lord," (1 Corinthians 12:5). As Lord of the Sabbath, Christ must also have entered into His rest, ceasing from His works as God did after creation. The reason for observing the Sabbath rests on this: it marks the day of our Lord's entrance into His rest. Our everlasting Sabbath in heaven will be an entrance into "the joy of thy Lord" (Matthew 25:21). Likewise, the comfort of the Sabbath now lies in communion with the Lord of the Sabbath as He rests. Therefore, as Christ is the Lord of the Sabbath, He must have entered into His rest, just as God did. The Apostle's argument here confirms this.

From all this, it becomes evident that the ceasing described in Hebrews 4:10 refers to Christ ceasing from His works and entering into His rest. With this established, we can see that the day of rest referred to in Psalm 95—"Today if ye will hear his voice"—is understood by the Apostle as a new Sabbath day, tied to Christ's rest as the seventh day was tied to God's rest.

Much more could be drawn from these two chapters to argue for the Christian Sabbath, but it is necessary to proceed to the main text. These reflections have been included because they will be useful later. Although this may seem like a digression, it is neither unnecessary nor irrelevant.

It is therefore clear that "Today if ye will hear his voice," refers to the Christian Sabbath day. The Apostle exhorts believers to observe this day in the house and worship of Christ, first using the words of the Prophet David in Hebrews 3:7, and then repeating the exhortation in his own words in Hebrews 4:12. The Apostle's commentary further develops David's words, drawing parallels to those who fell in the wilderness. David's Psalm describes the condition of those in Gospel times who abandon the ordinances and Sabbath of the New Testament, refusing to hear Christ's call to rest with Him on His appointed day, as being the same as those who tempted God in the wilderness by rejecting His promise to lead them into the land of Canaan and give them rest. God swore in His wrath that they would not enter into His rest.

Having completed his arguments and exhortations based on Psalm 95 in Hebrews 3 and 4, the Apostle transitions to another point. He continues to dissuade believers from abandoning Gospel worship and ordinances by explaining that Christ's coming necessitated a change in the priesthood and the law of ordinances. Christ is now "a priest forever after the order of Melchizedek," (Hebrews 5:6), not of Aaron. The Apostle begins this argument in Hebrews 5, develops it through chapters 7, 8, and 9, and concludes it in Hebrews 10:19, urging believers to resist apostasy.

The sixth chapter serves as a digression, beginning in Hebrews 5:11, where the Apostle rebukes the readers for their spiritual immaturity. He criticizes them, saying that although they ought to be teachers by now, they still require instruction in the basics of God's word. However, he resolves not to dwell on these elementary principles but to "go on unto perfection," (Hebrews 6:1) and address more challenging topics, "hard to be understood," (2 Peter 3:16). He explains that the recovery of those who have tasted the blessings of Christ's ordinances and house but have utterly fallen away would be in vain.

The Apostle tempers his stern rebuke with encouragement in Hebrews 6:9: "But, beloved, we are persuaded better things of you, and things that accompany salvation, though we thus speak." He seeks to comfort them and exhorts them to "show the same diligence to the full assurance of hope unto the end," (Hebrews 6:11) and to follow the example of those "who through faith and patience inherit the promises," (Hebrews 6:12).

In the words of this passage, the Apostle exhorts his readers to labor for a full assurance of hope by presenting the grounds for such assurance. He demonstrates this through the example of Abraham, the great model of believers, in two ways: *imitation* and *instruction*.

First, by way of imitation, the Apostle illustrates what God did for Abraham and what Abraham did in response, drawing parallels for believers to follow.

What God did for Abraham: God made a promise to Abraham, saying He would bless and multiply him. God confirmed this promise with an oath, swearing by Himself, as there was no greater by whom He could swear, thus providing Abraham with the greatest possible assurance.

What Abraham did and experienced in response: Abraham inherited the promise. This inheritance came after he had patiently endured.

The Apostle implies that if believers follow Abraham's example, *they too* will receive similar blessings, making Abraham's example a foundation for assurance of hope through imitation.

Second, by way of instruction, the Apostle explains that what God did for Abraham was not for him alone but for all believers, who are heirs of the same promise.

The nature and use of an oath among men: Men swear by someone greater than themselves. An oath provides confirmation, serving as the final resolution of disputes. God's purpose in making an oath to Abraham:

To demonstrate the unchanging nature of His counsel more abundantly to the heirs of the promise.

To provide strong consolation to believers, described as those who have fled for refuge to lay hold upon the hope set before them.

The Apostle highlights that this strong consolation is given through two unchangeable things—the promise and the oath—in which it is impossible for God to lie.

From this passage, several observations may be *made*:

First, the promises of the Gospel are obtained by inheritance. Abraham "inherited the promise," and all believers are likewise called "heirs of promise." They are begotten to a lively hope and an incorruptible inheritance (1 Peter 1:3–4). As Paul states in Acts 26:18, believers are brought "from darkness to light, and from the power of Satan unto God, that they may receive forgiveness of sins, and inheritance among them which are sanctified by faith that is in Christ." The ultimate reward will be the welcoming sentence from the Judge: "Come, ye blessed of my Father, inherit the kingdom prepared for you from the foundation of the world," (Matthew 25:34). This inheritance is secure, freely given by the Father, and the Gospel is His testament, promising the enjoyment of God Himself. Those who partake must therefore be His children through union with Christ. "And if children, then heirs; heirs of God, and joint-heirs with Christ," (Romans 8:17).

Second, faith and patience are necessary to enjoy this inheritance. The work of salvation is carried forward by the power of God's creative word, and "the word preached did not profit them, not being mixed with faith in them that heard it," (Hebrews 4:2). The Gospel is "the power of God unto salvation to everyone that believeth," (Romans 1:16). As God often fulfills His promises gradually rather than immediately, believers must exercise patience: "For ye have need of patience, that, after ye have done the will of God, ye might receive the promise," (Hebrews 10:36).

Third, the example of other believers provides significant encouragement for faith. Abraham's example is given as a foundation for confidence. Believers are called to "walk in the steps of that faith of our father Abraham," (Romans 4:12). David also found comfort in the testimony of others: "Our fathers trusted in thee: they trusted, and thou didst deliver them. They cried unto thee, and were delivered: they trusted in thee, and were not confounded," (Psalm 22:4–5). Faith is a great work, but it is shared among all believers: "Resist steadfast in the faith, knowing that the same afflictions are accomplished in your brethren that are in the world," (1 Peter 5:9). As Paul notes in Colossians 1:23, the Gospel has been preached "to every creature which is under heaven," encouraging steadfastness by reminding believers that they are not alone in their faith.

Fourth, oaths are lawful and, in some cases, a duty among Christians. God Himself swore an oath, and His example demonstrates the proper use of oaths: for confirmation and to resolve disputes. When God swears, He acts in a manner consistent with humanity but without sin, for Christ "was in all points tempted like as we are, yet without sin," (Hebrews 4:15). Scripture commands, "Thou shalt fear the Lord thy God, and serve him, and shalt swear by his name," (Deuteronomy 6:13). Jeremiah similarly states, "Thou shalt swear, The Lord liveth, in truth, in judgment, and in righteousness," (Jeremiah 4:2). These instructions clarify the prohibition of swearing in Matthew 5:33 and James 5:12: oaths should not be profane or frivolous but solemn, religious acts, sworn in God's name alone.

Fifth, believers have both the promise and the oath of God as a foundation for their confidence. God, in His love, does the utmost for His people. As the Psalmist declares, "Thine arrows are sharp in the heart of the king's enemies; whereby the people fall under thee," (Psalm 45:5). Similarly, in confirming His promises, "because he could swear by no greater, he sware by himself," (Hebrews 6:13). If we remain unbelieving despite all that God has done and said, we are indeed guilty of great sin, as Jesus declared: "Of sin, because they believe not on me," (John 16:9).

Sixth, there is often a conflict between God and the doubting soul of a believer. Believers may be full of disputes and doubts, which lead to discomfort and unrest. To resolve this, God gives His promise and oath to bring an end to such inner strife: "That by two immutable things, in which it was impossible for God to lie, we might have a strong consolation," (Hebrews 6:18).

Although much more could be drawn from this passage, this final point serves as the central observation for the present consideration.

Seventhly, the promise that the Lord confirmed by an oath to Abraham was also confirmed to *all* believers, extending to the end of the world. Abraham is presented here as a pattern, and all believers are considered to inherit the promise *made to him*, sharing in it as his heirs. The Apostle makes this clear, stating that what God did for Abraham—confirming the promise to bless and multiply him with an oath—was done not only for Abraham but to demonstrate the unchanging nature of His counsel to all the heirs of the promise. The purpose was to provide strong consolation to us, the believers of the New Testament. If the promise confirmed to Abraham had not also been intended for us, its confirmation would not provide us with any comfort, nor could we be called heirs of that promise.

For further evidence, consider Galatians 3:29: "If ye be Christ's, then are ye Abraham's seed, and heirs according to the promise." This verse shows that what we have in Christ, we receive as Abraham's seed and as heirs with him of the same promise. Conversely, what we have as Abraham's seed, we have through Christ. Thus, the promise to Abraham serves as a *summary* of the Gospel. As Luke 1:55, 72–73 states, the coming of Christ fulfilled the oath of God to Abraham: "He hath holpen his servant Israel, in remembrance of his mercy; as he spake to our fathers, to Abraham, and to his seed forever. To perform the mercy promised to our fathers, and to remember his holy covenant; the oath which he sware to our father Abraham." Through Christ, we are delivered from the hands of our enemies to serve God without fear, in holiness and righteousness all our days.

This is further supported by the fact that believers, both Jews and Gentiles, are called Abraham's seed, making them recipients of the promise. Galatians 3:16 states: "To Abraham and his seed were the promises made. He saith not, And to seeds, as of many; but as of one, And to thy seed, which is Christ." The covenant, confirmed by God in Christ 430 years before the law, could not be annulled by the law. The "one seed," Christ, does not refer solely to Christ personally but to Christ in His mystical body, which includes all believers. As 1 Corinthians 12:12 says: "For as the body is one, and hath many members, and all the members of that one body, being many, are one body: so also is Christ." This body, composed of Jews and Gentiles, is one seed. The Apostle makes this clear by referring to the covenant as "confirmed in Christ" to believers united to Him, both Jews and Gentiles. Therefore, the promise to Abraham was confirmed to all believers as his seed.

Romans 4:16 provides further evidence: "Therefore it is of faith, that it might be by grace; to the end the promise might be sure to all the seed; not to that only which is of the law, but to that also which is of the faith of Abraham; who is the father of us all."

Psalm 105:6–10 further illustrates this: "O ye seed of Abraham his servant, ye children of Jacob his chosen. He hath remembered his covenant forever, the word which he commanded to a thousand generations; which covenant he made with Abraham, and his oath unto Isaac; and confirmed the same unto Jacob for a law, and to Israel for an everlasting covenant." Even the promise concerning the land of Canaan, often viewed as limited to the Old Testament, is described as "a covenant forever" and "an everlasting possession," in Genesis 17:8: "I will give unto thee, and to thy seed after thee, the land wherein thou art a stranger, all the land of Canaan, for an everlasting possession; and I will be their God." This must extend to the New Testament era, as the literal possession of Canaan ceased long ago for Abraham's natural descendants.

The Apostle, referencing Genesis 22:16–17, connects this promise to the Gospel: "By myself have I sworn, saith the Lord, for because thou hast done this thing, and hast not withheld thy son, thine only son: That in blessing I will bless thee, and in multiplying I will multiply thy seed as the stars of the heaven, and as the sand which is upon the sea shore; and thy seed shall possess the gate of his enemies." This includes the spiritual blessings of the heavenly Canaan, *represented* by the earthly Canaan.

Canaan, and its good things, served as a *type* of the spiritual blessings of the New Testament Church and heaven itself. Ezekiel 47:22 speaks of the New Testament Church under the type of Canaan, declaring: "The strangers shall have inheritance with you among the tribes of Israel." Isaiah 65:9 similarly describes it: "Mine elect shall inherit it, and my servants shall dwell there."

Abraham, by faith, embraced this promise as referring not only to earthly but also heavenly inheritance. Hebrews 11:8–10 explains that he sojourned in the land of promise "as in a strange country," because "he looked for a city which hath foundations, whose builder and maker is God." Verses 13–16 elaborate that Abraham and his descendants "confessed that they were strangers and pilgrims on the earth," seeking "a better country, that is, an heavenly."

God, fulfilling this promise, declared Himself to be their God, a fulfillment far surpassing a mere earthly inheritance. Deuteronomy 26:1–11 ties the acknowledgment of Canaan's blessings to spiritual realities, as their gratitude for temporal blessings typified thankfulness for spiritual blessings.

Esau is condemned as "a profane person" for selling his birthright, which included not only earthly but spiritual blessings. Hebrews 12:16 likens this to those who abandon Gospel privileges for worldly gain, showing the *spiritual* nature of the promise.

Hebrews 3 and 4 clarify that God's promise of rest in Canaan included spiritual rest in Christ. The Gospel promise of rest in God through Christ was preached to Israel in the wilderness. When God swore that the rebellious Israelites would not enter His rest, it referred to both the earthly and spiritual Canaan, as confirmed by the Apostle's interpretation of Psalm 95. Thus, the promise concerning Canaan encompasses the spiritual blessings of the Gospel and the heavenly inheritance.

In Hebrews 3:17, the Apostle writes, "With whom was he grieved forty years? was it not with them that sinned, whose carcasses fell in the wilderness?" The phrase should be more accurately rendered as, "Whom did He disdain for forty years?" The Greek term προσώχθισε (*prosōchthise*) is consistently used in Scripture to mean "to abominate" or "to reject," as one would reject something unclean, hateful, or profane. Examples of this usage include Deuteronomy 7:26:

"Thou shalt utterly detest it, and thou shalt utterly abhor it, for it is an accursed thing"; 2 Chronicles 21:6: "The king's word was abominable unto Joab"; Psalm 36:4: "He abhorreth not evil"; and Leviticus 26:15, 18, 25. The Hebrew term קָטַר (*qattar*), found in Psalm 95, is similarly translated as "I had in disdain," as Junius and Montanus render it.

This term holds great significance, as it emphasizes God's withdrawal of favor from His people and His disdain for their sin, leading Him to keep them at a distance for forty years in the wilderness. This disdain extended not only to earthly blessings but also to spiritual enjoyments, for He swore that they would not "enter into His rest." A similar divine response is seen in Psalm 106:40: "The wrath of the Lord was kindled against his people, insomuch that he abhorred his own inheritance."

Thus, the proper rendering of Hebrews 3:17 is, "Whom did He hold in disdain for forty years? Was it not them that sinned, whose carcasses fell in the wilderness?" The Apostle continues in verse 18: "And to whom sware he that they should not enter into his rest, but to them that believed not?" and concludes in verse 19: "So we see that they could not enter in because of unbelief." In Hebrews 4:1, the Apostle applies this lesson: "Let us therefore fear, lest, a promise being left us of entering into his rest, any of you should seem to come short of it. For unto us was the gospel preached, as well as unto them: but the word preached did not profit them, not being mixed with faith in them that heard it."

The Apostle equates their case with ours, stating that the Gospel was preached to them as it is to us. The outcomes, however, depend on whether the word is *mixed with faith*. The failure of the word to profit them serves as a warning that it may likewise fail to profit us.

To understand the Apostle's teaching here, particularly the assertion that the offer of Canaan was a form of Gospel preaching, we must revisit the earlier points regarding the Apostle's purpose in this epistle. First, he addressed this letter to those who professed faith in Christ but were abandoning the worship of the New Testament. A primary aim of the epistle is to prevent and cure this apostasy. The Apostle reminds them that "the Lord's people are his house," (Hebrews 3:6) and exhorts them, using the words of the Holy Spirit, to hear Christ's voice, who as the "Apostle and High Priest of our profession," calls them to celebrate His day of rest in His house and worship under the Gospel.

Second, believers are described as God's house in two distinct ways.

1. As members of Christ's mystical body, believers are part of the invisible Church and, as such, are His house. Just as every drop of water is part of the sea, so every individual believer is part of God's house (Ephesians 3:17, John 14:23, 1 Corinthians 6:19, 1 John 4:16).

2. As members of a ministerial body, or the visible Church, believers are His house in a corporate sense. In this way, the Church and its ordinances serve as, the means by which believers experience communion with Christ. The visible Church is therefore called the, "body of Christ" (1 Corinthians 12:27) and His "house" (Ephesians 2:22).

As believers, we enter into God's rest in these two ways.

1. Personally, as individuals united to Christ by faith. 2. Publicly, through the worship and ordinances of His house, particularly in the sanctification of His Sabbaths. These are ordained means by which personal faith is strengthened, and God's rest is more fully enjoyed. The Apostle focuses primarily on this second capacity, warning against forsaking the Gospel's worship and ordinances. He writes, "Take heed, brethren, lest there be in any of you an evil heart of unbelief, in departing from the living God," (Hebrews 3:12). He emphasizes that forsaking worship is tantamount to rejecting the rest offered in the Gospel, just as Israel rejected the rest offered in Canaan. If they refuse, God will "swear in his wrath" that they shall not enter His rest.

While every true believer enjoys rest in God through Christ by faith—a rest they will never fully lose—they may fall short of the fuller experience of this rest provided in the public worship of God's house. Such neglect, the Apostle warns, is a "departure from the living God" in a partial, though not total, sense. This neglect may obscure the believer's personal rest to others and even to their own soul, as indicated in Hebrews 4:1: "Lest any of you should seem to come short of it."

This parallel is seen in those who fell in the wilderness. While they did not enter Canaan, many still entered heaven and enjoyed rest in God by faith. Moses, Aaron, and Miriam were among them, as expressed in the prayer of Moses: "Lord, thou hast been our dwelling place in all generations," (Psalm 90:1). Nevertheless, their refusal to enter Canaan is called apostasy from God (Numbers 14:9), where Caleb warns, "Be not ye apostates from the Lord," (μὴ ἀποστατεῖτε in the Septuagint), the same word the Apostle employs here.

The Apostle's reasoning in Hebrews 4:2, "For unto us was the gospel preached, as well as unto them," assumes that the gospel was preached to the Israelites in the wilderness just as it is preached to us. The gospel is a promise of rest in God, through Christ, by faith, as Jesus stated: "Take my yoke upon you, and learn of me; and ye shall find rest unto your souls," (Matthew 11:29). A part of this rest is the enjoyment of God's rest in the service of His house on His appointed day. Just as believers now experience this rest through the ordinances and Sabbath of the New Testament, the Israelites experienced it through the Sabbaths and ordinances of the Old Testament, with Canaan and its blessings, along with their conquest of enemies and protection from them, being a part of that rest. Thus, God's offer of Canaan to Israel was an offer to enter His rest and, therefore, a preaching of the gospel.

In the administration of the covenant of grace under the Old Testament, God used types and shadows, including the type of Canaan. Their passage from Egypt, crossing the Red Sea, and being sustained by water from the rock in the wilderness were all types. Yet, in these types, the Israelites experienced the same communion with God in Christ as believers now experience through New Testament ordinances like baptism and the Lord's Supper. As Paul writes, "That Rock was Christ," (1 Corinthians 10:4), just as the bread in the Lord's Supper is His body. The same chapter of 1 Corinthians also demonstrates that their sins and punishments were comparable to ours, as Psalm 95 underscores.

The conquest of Canaan itself can be considered a *church action*. This conclusion arises not only because they "subdued kingdoms by faith," (Hebrews 11:33) but also because the conquest was the execution of an *anathema*—a sentence of destruction pronounced by God. The inhabitants were not merely defeated as enemies according to natural law but were treated as accursed things. Such actions required a consecrated people to whom these accursed things were dedicated for destruction. As Deuteronomy 20:10–17 outlines, Israel was to treat distant cities differently from the Canaanite cities. While they could make peace with distant cities and spare some lives if they were conquered, God commanded, "Thou shalt save alive nothing that breatheth; but thou shalt utterly destroy them," in Canaan, using the Hebrew term חרם (*cherem*), meaning "devote them" or "anathematize them."

This consecration explains why the entire congregation was held accountable for Achan's sin in taking the accursed thing (Joshua 7:1). The Geneva Bible aptly translates this as "the excommunicate thing." The conquest of Jericho was a church action requiring communal vigilance. When Achan broke rank and stole, the whole congregation suffered the consequences. Similarly, in Joshua 22, when the tribes of Reuben, Gad, and the half-tribe of Manasseh built an altar, the congregation feared it might signify idolatry. They acted with the same vigilance, citing examples like Achan and the sin at Peor, where the sin of a few brought judgment on all.

The promise of Canaan, then, was a *gospel* promise. Abraham regarded it as such, and his spiritual seed enjoyed not only the earthly Canaan but also the heavenly Canaan, even under the Old Testament. The heavenly Canaan continues to exist and will be enjoyed by believers of all generations, demonstrating that the promise of Canaan was intended for the New Testament Church as well, making it an everlasting possession.

The Lord confirmed His gospel promise by singling out Abraham as a pattern and extending that promise to his spiritual seed. God has often acted in this manner, as seen with Jacob. When God promised victory over enemies through prayer, He gave the name "Israel" to Jacob, signifying his prevailing with God. Believers now claim that privilege and are called "the Israel of God" (Galatians 6:16): "Peace be on them, and on the Israel of God." Similarly, when Christ gave the keys of the kingdom of heaven, He gave them to Peter, explaining his new name, saying, "Thou art Peter, and upon this rock I will build my church," (Matthew 16:18). Believers now claim this church authority, derived from Peter's role as a confessor and a "stone" in the house of God. Church officers, being particularly entrusted with church authority, possess a greater share of this power. Likewise, God singled out Abraham and confirmed His promises to him for all believers, giving him the name Abraham to signify his role as the father of many nations.

The Apostle, quoting Genesis 22:16–17, highlights the promise made to Abraham: "By myself have I sworn, saith the Lord, for because thou hast done this thing, and hast not withheld thy son, thine only son: That in blessing I will bless thee, and in multiplying I will multiply thy seed as the stars of the heaven, and as the sand which is upon the sea shore; and thy seed shall possess the gate of his enemies." While the Apostle focuses on the manner of God's confirmation by an oath, the full scope of the promise is seen throughout Genesis, especially chapters 12, 17, and 22.

The promise includes four main aspects. First, God promised to bless Abraham and all believers with all spiritual blessings in Christ, as heirs and children of God. Romans 9:7 explains: "Neither, because they are the seed of Abraham, are they all children: but, In Isaac shall thy seed be called." The blessing is further clarified in Galatians 3:8–9: "The scripture, foreseeing that God would justify the heathen through faith, preached before the gospel unto Abraham, saying, In thee shall all nations be blessed. So then they which be of faith are blessed with faithful Abraham." All blessings in Christ are encompassed in this promise, which *summarizes* the gospel.

Second, the promise includes a particular blessing for Abraham and his spiritual descendants: they would be blessings themselves, especially to their families and even to nations. Genesis 12:2–3 declares: "I will bless thee, and make thy name great; and thou shalt be a blessing: And I will bless them that bless thee, and curse him that curseth thee: and in thee shall all families of the earth be blessed." This promise was explained by Peter in Acts 3:25–26: "Ye are the children of the prophets, and of the covenant which God made with our fathers, saying unto Abraham, And in thy seed shall all the kindreds of the earth be blessed. Unto you first God, having raised up his Son Jesus, sent him to bless you."

This blessing extends not only to Abraham's physical descendants but also to all families of the earth. It encompasses Christ's coming, for all we receive from Abraham is through Christ. Moreover, it signifies that believers themselves will be blessings in their generations. The inclusion of families in this promise is clear from the specific language: "all the families of the earth shall be blessed." This covenantal blessing applies to believers and their households, demonstrating God's continuing care for *the families* of His people.

The meaning is this: when the Lord bestows mercy and salvation upon humanity, He does so not based on human merit, either actual or foreseen, but according to His own free choice. In His covenant with Abraham, God reveals that His election will not be evenly distributed across the world but will be carried out by *families* and *nations*. Thus, God often grants elect children to elect parents and clusters His saints together in certain places and communities rather than distributing them equally across the world. Without this divine arrangement, neither Abraham nor believers could be called blessings in spiritual matters to their *families* or *communities*. However, they are blessings precisely because God chooses to bless His elect through them: "He hath blessed us according as he hath chosen us," (Ephesians 1:3-4).

For further proof, this pattern is evident in the course of history. God's people are not equally distributed across all places but are often found concentrated in certain families or nations. This does not happen by chance but because of God's deliberate choice. He declares Himself to be "a God to believers and their seed in their generations," making them blessings to their children, neighbors, and acquaintances. This is not merely the result of good upbringing or natural means, although proper education and example greatly influence young hearts toward Christ. Rather, it is due to a special word of promise, a creative act of God, which grants efficacy to the means employed. Without this divine promise—first given to Abraham and his seed—education and other efforts would not have such power to turn sinners to God.

Scripture offers further evidence for this truth. Psalm 105 declares that God's covenant with Abraham is "a word which he hath commanded to a thousand generations," indicating that this promise blesses posterity from generation to generation. Genesis 17:7 states: "I will establish my covenant between me and thee, and thy seed after thee in their generations, to be a God unto thee, and to thy seed after thee."

This truth is further illustrated in Luke 19:9, where Jesus, upon Zacchaeus's conversion, declares: "This day is salvation come to this house, forasmuch as he also is a son of Abraham." Salvation was not limited to Zacchaeus's soul but extended to his household, consistent with God's promise to Abraham. Similarly, Paul tells the jailer in Acts 16:31, "Believe on the Lord Jesus Christ, and thou shalt be saved, and thy house," underscoring the promise that God blesses believers and their families.

In Romans 11:16, Paul uses the metaphor of the root and branches to explain this covenant blessing. He writes: "For if the firstfruit be holy, the lump is also holy: and if the root be holy, so are the branches." Here, Abraham and the patriarchs are likened to a holy root, from which blessings flow to their descendants. Verse 28 further explains: "As concerning the gospel, they are enemies for your sakes: but as touching the election, they are beloved for the fathers' sakes. For the gifts and calling of God are without repentance." Though the Jews were broken off from this holy root due to unbelief, Gentiles were grafted in, and the Jews will one day be restored for the sake of the fathers. This demonstrates that the covenant promise to Abraham remains active across generations.

Paul also declares in 1 Corinthians 7:14, "The unbelieving husband is sanctified by the wife, and the unbelieving wife is sanctified by the husband: else were your children unclean; but now are they holy." Similarly, Peter exhorts the Jews in Acts 2:38–39 to repent and be baptized, "for the promise is unto you, and to your children, and to all that are afar off, even as many as the Lord our God shall call."

The covenant with Abraham also reveals its generational blessing through the ordinance of circumcision, which was applied to infants as a sign and seal of God's promise. Circumcision symbolized the *circumcision of the heart* that God promises for the children of His people. This unique aspect of God's covenant with Abraham expands upon the earlier promises given to the Church before him. Abraham is called "the father of all them that believe", (Romans 4:11) because he received this promise and its seal, which secured blessings for his spiritual descendants.

Some may object, saying that godly parents often have ungodly children, and sometimes the children of ungodly parents become believers. How, then, can a believer be a blessing to their family? Or how is God's election carried through families as described?

To this, I answer: while God makes His people blessings, the effect of this blessing is sometimes hindered by human sin. God's blessings, though holy and powerful, do not always take effect because of the willful rejection or sinfulness of individuals. For example, God promises to bless His Word, ensuring His presence in and through it. However, the Word is not always effective in those who hear it, due to their *unbelief*. This principle also applies to the blessings promised to families. God, in His wisdom, chooses to work through families, but individual rebellion may limit the manifestation of His blessings within a given generation.

The Apostle highlights a significant truth about God's promises to Abraham and his seed, emphasizing that God's covenant and actions were not confined to history but have enduring implications for His people throughout time. This is evident in the way the Apostle relates the Gospel promises to Abraham's covenant, particularly as he notes that God's blessings and covenant were given with an eye toward their fulfillment in the New Testament.

First, the Apostle shows that the Gospel was preached to both *us and them*, meaning the Israelites under the Old Testament and believers now. This shows that the promise of rest in God through Christ, as expressed in

Matthew 11:29, has been consistent across the ages. The enjoyment of rest in the worship of God's house and on His Sabbath day was part of the Gospel message, both in the ordinances of the Old Testament and in those of the New. The land of Canaan, its blessings, and the subjugation of enemies served as a type, pointing forward to the greater spiritual realities fulfilled in Christ. Thus, God's offer of Canaan to Israel symbolized an entrance into His rest, representing the Gospel proclaimed in types and shadows.

God has always administered His covenant of grace through types and symbols under the Old Testament. For instance, the Israelites' passage through the Red Sea and the provision of water from the rock in the wilderness were *types* of Gospel blessings. As Paul writes, "That Rock was Christ," (1 Corinthians 10:4). Similarly, the conquest of Canaan was not merely a political or natural event but a sacred act connected to God's covenant promises, just as baptism and the Lord's Supper signify participation in Christ now. In this way, the types of the Old Testament reveal the *same* spiritual blessings we enjoy under the New Testament.

The conquest of Canaan itself was a church action, evidenced by the unique commands God gave to Israel regarding the destruction of the Canaanites. In Deuteronomy 20:10-18, God distinguishes between nations far from Israel and the inhabitants of Canaan. While Israel could make peace with distant nations, they were commanded to utterly destroy the Canaanites as accursed, devoting them to God. This judgment was not a natural act of war but a sacred execution of God's anathema upon those people. For this reason, when Achan sinned by taking from the accursed things, the entire congregation was guilty, as they were bound together in a communal obligation to uphold God's commands (Joshua 7:1).

The same communal principle is evident when Israel dealt with the altar built by the tribes of Reuben, Gad, and Manasseh. The congregation acted to preserve purity in worship, paralleling their responsibility in other cases of communal sin, such as the sins of Achan and the incident at Peor (Joshua 22:10-34). These examples show that Israel's actions were not merely civil or political but were tied to their identity as God's covenant people, responsible for preserving His worship and laws.

From this, it is clear that the promise of Canaan to Abraham and his seed was a Gospel promise. Abraham understood this promise as encompassing not only earthly blessings but also spiritual and eternal blessings. The Apostle demonstrates this by pointing out that Abraham believed in God's promise of an innumerable seed and was justified by faith (Genesis 15:5-6; Romans 4:3). This faith extended beyond the physical descendants of Abraham to include believing Gentiles, as Paul explains in Romans 4:13-17. Thus, the promise that Abraham would be the heir of the world includes the expansion of God's kingdom through the multiplication of believers.

The fulfillment of this promise involves the spread of the Gospel and the ultimate triumph of Christ's kingdom. Daniel 2 describes the kingdom of Christ as a *stone* that grows into a mountain and fills the whole earth, symbolizing the global spread of the Gospel. Similarly, Jesus compares the kingdom to a mustard seed that grows into a large tree and to leaven, that spreads throughout the dough (Matthew 13:31-33). Through the multiplication of Abraham's spiritual seed, the knowledge of Christ will eventually fill the earth, as foretold in Romans 4:13 and Psalm 47.

Furthermore, the promise that Abraham's seed would "possess the gate of his enemies," (Genesis 22:17) signifies the ultimate victory of God's people over their adversaries. Gates in ancient times symbolized power and authority, as they were places of judgment and decision-making (Amos 5:15; Deuteronomy 16:18). This promise is fulfilled in Christ's kingdom, as seen in passages like Revelation 11:15: "The kingdoms of this world are become the kingdoms of our Lord, and of his Christ; and he shall reign forever and ever." The dominion and authority granted to Christ and His people are further illustrated in Daniel 7:18-28, where the saints are given the kingdom and all dominions serve and obey God.

Psalm 105 further reinforces these truths, recounting God's faithfulness to His covenant with Abraham. This psalm, written during the time of David, recalls how God delivered Israel from Egypt, preserved them in the wilderness, and gave them the land of Canaan. These historical events are presented as types, foreshadowing the greater spiritual deliverance and inheritance that God provides through Christ. The psalmist declares that God remembered His holy promise to Abraham and fulfilled it, not only in history but also in anticipation of future blessings under the Gospel.

The psalmist in Psalm 78 refers to these historical events as "parables" and "dark sayings" (Psalm 78:1-2), indicating that they were not merely historical accounts but also carried deeper spiritual meanings. Jesus Himself applies this idea in Matthew 13:35, showing that the psalm contains prophetic truths about His work and the expansion of His kingdom. Likewise, Psalm 105 serves as a prophecy, revealing that the victories and blessings experienced by Israel under the Old Testament were *types* of the ultimate triumph of Christ's kingdom.

In this way, the promise to Abraham, confirmed through God's oath, encompasses spiritual blessings for all believers, the multiplication of God's people, their ultimate victory over their enemies, and the expansion of Christ's kingdom to fill the earth. These promises, though given in types and shadows under the Old Testament, find their ultimate fulfillment in Christ and His church under the New Testament. Through these truths, we see the immutability of God's counsel and His faithfulness to His covenant with Abraham and his seed.

From Psalm 105, it becomes clear that the conquest of the world by the kingdom of Christ is part of the promise made to Abraham and his seed. "Remember his marvellous works that he hath done; his wonders, and the judgments of his mouth; O ye seed of Abraham his servant, ye children of Jacob his chosen," (Psalm 105:5-6). This promise is evident not only in Genesis 22:16, where it is said, "Thy seed shall possess the gate of his enemies," but also in Genesis 17:8: "I will give to thee and to thy seed after thee, the land wherein thou art a stranger, all the land of Canaan, for an everlasting possession, and I will be their God." To understand this further—that the conquest promised in these verses applies to Abraham's seed—consider the following:

First, we have already established that the promise of Canaan, as an everlasting possession, was a Gospel promise meant to be fulfilled in the New Testament era. The spiritual blessings of the heavenly Canaan, of which the earthly Canaan and its blessings were types, include the multiplication of Abraham's spiritual seed. This multiplication will ultimately lead to the world being filled with and subdued to Christ. If the spiritual blessings of the heavenly Canaan are part of this promise, the conquest of the world by Abraham's spiritual seed is also necessarily included. This conquest is a spiritual one, achieved through the sword of the Spirit, the Word of God, and it includes the victory over sin and the enjoyment of the heavenly blessings of Christ's kingdom. What God accomplished for Abraham's seed in the earthly Canaan serves as a type of this greater spiritual conquest. "He hath remembered his covenant for ever, the word which he commanded to a thousand generations. Which covenant he made with Abraham, and his oath unto Isaac; And confirmed the same unto Jacob for a law, and to Israel for an everlasting covenant: Saying, Unto thee will I give the land of Canaan, the lot of your inheritance," (Psa. 105:8-11).

Secondly, it is undeniable that Abraham's seed possessed the gates of their enemies during the conquest of the earthly Canaan. This establishes that Genesis 22:16 (concerning the possession of the enemy's gate) and Genesis 17:8 (about Canaan as an everlasting possession) are parallel promises addressing the same ultimate purpose. The Apostle, in referencing the oath of God in Genesis 22:16, links the fulfillment of this promise to the times of the New Testament. Consequently, it should be evident that the possession of the gates of their enemies in the earthly Canaan typifies what Abraham's spiritual seed will achieve over their spiritual enemies in the New Testament era.

Thirdly, consider Genesis 9:26-27, where a promise is made to Shem and Japheth that mirrors the promises to Abraham and his seed. "Blessed be the Lord God of Shem; and Canaan shall be his servant. God shall enlarge Japheth, and he shall dwell in the tents of Shem; and Canaan shall be his servant." Shem's dominion over Canaan was fulfilled in the conquest of Canaan by Abraham's descendants, who were of Shem's lineage. Japheth's dwelling in the tents of Shem, however, awaits fulfillment in the New Testament, when Jews and Gentiles are united as one Church. Shem and Japheth symbolize the Church of the New Testament, where natural distinctions of lineage fade, and Canaan represents the wicked of the world who will ultimately serve the Church. In this way, when God renewed the promise to Abraham, adding the method of its fulfillment—blessing and multiplying his seed—it reflected the same truth: that Abraham and his seed would inherit the world, fill it, and rule over it.

Further evidence comes from Zechariah 14:21, which speaks of the fulfillment of this promise in the latter days: "In that day there shall be no more the Canaanite in the house of the Lord of Hosts." Here, "Canaanite" symbolizes the wicked or worldly, paralleling Revelation 21:27, which declares, "There shall in no wise enter into it anything that defileth, neither whatsoever worketh abomination, or maketh a lie; but they which are written in the Lamb's book of life."

Additionally, consider the observation regarding Abraham's victory over four kings in Genesis 14. These kings—Amraphel, Arioch, Chedorlaomer, and Tidal—symbolize the four great monarchies later depicted in Nebuchadnezzar's image in Daniel 2. Abraham's conquest foreshadowed how his spiritual seed, the saints, would eventually break these earthly powers and inherit their dominion (Daniel 2:44).

Thus, the promise to Abraham and his seed encompasses four significant blessings:

1. God would bless Abraham and, through him, all believers with spiritual blessings in Christ.

2. Believers would become blessings to their families, neighbors, and nations.

3. God would multiply Abraham's spiritual seed, filling and subduing the world to Christ's kingdom.

4. Abraham's seed would possess the gates of their enemies, symbolizing the ultimate victory of Christ's kingdom.

These promises, which include the establishment, growth, and triumph of *Christ's* kingdom, are part of the Gospel. This is why it is called "the Gospel of the kingdom," offering the glad tidings of salvation through Christ and the assurance of the saints' inheritance and victory.

The Apostle explains that these promises were given to Abraham as a pattern for all believers, to show the immutability of God's counsel to the heirs of promise and to strengthen their faith. By structuring His work across ages and generations, God provided types and examples through His dealings with Abraham and Israel, enabling believers to trust in His faithfulness. David expressed this same trust in Psalm 22:4-5: "Our fathers trusted in thee: they trusted, and thou didst deliver them. They cried unto thee, and were delivered: they trusted in thee, and were not confounded."

Thus, the promises given to Abraham were not only historical blessings but enduring assurances of God's covenant faithfulness, meant to comfort and strengthen the faith of His people across all generations.

The second reason for this method of God's blessing lies in the clarity and certainty it provides to His people. Instead of conveying His mind through extensive written descriptions, which could become subject to varying interpretations across languages, ages, and nations, He chose to establish *one clear pattern* in Abraham. This approach allows all generations to understand His purposes through observable realities rather than words alone, reducing misunderstandings. For example, God first demonstrated the privilege and power of overcoming enemies through prayer by giving this to Jacob (Genesis 32) when He renamed him Israel, setting a precedent for all His people to follow.

The question arises: why does God, who distributes blessings according to His free election, restrict His choice to families and nations, instead of evenly distributing His people across the world? Several reasons can be given.

1. To Glorify Himself Through Weakness: God delights in bringing glory to Himself by choosing what is small and seemingly insignificant. Just as He selects the weak and humble over the mighty, He also includes children in His kingdom. Jesus said, "Of such is the kingdom of God," (Mark 10:14). This means not that children qualify by their innocence, but that they are *part* of His kingdom. Jesus' statement shows that children can receive His blessings just as adults do, emphasizing that entering His kingdom involves passivity and dependence, similar to how children receive care. In this way, the promise that families of the righteous will be blessed is a key part of the Gospel.

2. To Mirror Redemption Through Christ: God's blessings through families highlight how Christ, the second Adam, brings life in contrast to the death brought by the first Adam. In Adam, all die, but in Christ, all are made alive (1 Corinthians 15:22). Becoming children of the second Adam is founded on God's election, as Ephesians 1:4 declares: "He hath chosen us in him, having predestinated us unto the adoption of children by Jesus Christ." Though children of believers are born under wrath by nature, God's promise confines His election to ordinarily include *elect* children in *elect* families.

3. Out of Love for the Parents: God's love for His elect parents moves Him to bless their children, recognizing how deeply parents cherish their children's salvation. Scripture affirms this: "Because he loved thy fathers, therefore he chose their seed after them," (Deuteronomy 4:37). Romans 11:28 likewise speaks of God's regard for the descendants of the faithful.

4. To Provide Godly Upbringing: God places elect children in families where they will be raised in His fear. For example, Isaac could not have received such godly training outside Abraham's household, of which God said, "I know him, that he will command his children and his household after him, and they shall keep the way of the Lord," (Genesis 18:19). Without this focus on families, children would lack essential guidance, and the advantages of a godly upbringing would be lost. Families of believers, which once served as individual churches, continue to receive His blessing even now.

5. To Multiply the Kingdom: Restricting His election to families and nations serves as the most effective way to expand His kingdom. By making believers blessings, He laid the foundation for the kingdom's growth, likened to leaven that permeates the whole world (Matthew 13:33). Through godly upbringing and the witness of believers, successive generations increase in faith and knowledge, ensuring that "the earth shall be full of the knowledge of the Lord, as the waters cover the sea," (Isaiah 11:9). Had God scattered His elect evenly across the globe, this growth would have been hindered. Instead, by grouping His people, He ensures they edify one another and build upon the faith of previous generations.

Additionally, this method aligns with God's design under the New Testament: to make His truth accessible to His people through ordinary means. Unlike in the Old Testament, where prophets were necessary, God now allows believers to search and understand Scripture through ordinary gifts and study.

Why Multiply the Spiritual Seed? The answer is simple: to fulfill His promise to Abraham that his seed would fill the world and possess the gates of their enemies. Though God could accomplish this through force, He prefers to use righteous means. His kingdom must be established in righteousness, not through violence. As Psalm 45:6 states, "The scepter of thy kingdom is a right scepter." This righteous approach aligns with His original mandate to humanity: "Be fruitful, and multiply, and replenish the earth, and subdue it," (Genesis 1:28). Though the fall has altered humanity's nature, this dominion remains, as reaffirmed to Noah: "Into your hand are they delivered," (Genesis 9:2).

However, while the saints are not entitled by their faith to seize the possessions of their enemies through force, God promises that through *spiritual* means, they will ultimately inherit the earth. This ensures that the kingdom of Christ grows according to principles of righteousness, bringing glory to God and fulfilling His promises to Abraham and his seed.

The objection might arise that when the nations in the Promised Land were destroyed by the Church of God, the Israelites did not act in accordance with the common rules of righteousness among men. Specifically, it could be argued that Israel had no natural or reasonable claim to that land.

To this, I respond: what the Israelites did was by *direct* revelation and command from God. When God decided to establish a national Church and make the land possessed by His people a holy land, He exercised His sovereign prerogative. When the iniquity of the previous inhabitants was complete, He devoted them to destruction, declaring them accursed. While God justly passed this sentence upon them for their sins, His people, by His command, executed that judgment. However, such revelations and commands are not to be expected in the times of the New Testament. Although there remain execrable things within the Church that are to be purged out by God's institution, these actions pertain to a spiritual, not a physical, conquest. The possession of an earthly Canaan was a type of a greater spiritual reality. Its antitype is not the casting out of wicked people from nations or the world but the excommunication of unrepentant sinners from the Church. In this way, no physical or political actions are warranted by the Church as such.

Although God's people may have just cause to make war against Antichrist and his followers, such conflicts will arise from natural and civil matters—defending liberties invaded by those forces—not as a religious mandate.

God's promise to Abraham's seed to "possess the gate of their enemies," (Genesis 22:17) is fulfilled through multiplying His people. By blessing and increasing them, He ensures they naturally obtain dominion and power, not by force, but by virtue of their sheer numbers and the just principles of governance. As Isaiah 2:3-4 foretells, in the last days, when "the mountain of the Lord's house," (the Church) is established above all others, nations will cease learning war, and weapons will be repurposed for peace.

The Lord will accomplish this by both diminishing the numbers of the wicked and multiplying His people. Over time, the seed of Abraham will become so numerous that, by the natural course of righteousness and justice, they will possess the gates of their enemies. This explains why God so greatly multiplies the spiritual seed of Abraham.

Regarding the fourth question—why the power of Abraham's seed to possess their enemies' gates is part of God's promise—I point to the promise made to Adam and Eve. From the beginning, God promised the righteous would triumph over the wicked. In Genesis 3:15, He declared, "The seed of the woman shall bruise the serpent's head." This was renewed to Noah's sons, Shem and Japheth, in Genesis 9:27, "God shall enlarge Japheth, and he shall dwell in the tents of Shem; and Canaan shall be his servant." This means that Jews and Gentiles will form one Church, with the wicked of the world under their authority. Thus, Abraham's seed inheriting this power is a reaffirmation of God's original covenantal promise, with the addition of revealing how this power would be obtained.

Objection: Christ's Kingdom is Not of This World. An objection might be raised from Christ's own words, "My kingdom is not of this world," (John 18:36). How, then, can it be said that His saints will inherit such dominion and power, as described in Daniel 7:27, "The kingdom and dominion, and the greatness of the kingdom under the whole heaven, shall be given to the people of the saints of the most High"? Or in Revelation 11:15, "The kingdoms of this world are become the kingdoms of our Lord, and of his Christ"?

I answer: while Christ's kingdom is indeed "not of this world," it is still true that the kingdoms of this world will become His. His kingdom remains spiritual and heavenly in its nature, laws, power, and ends. Unlike the kingdoms of this world, which are temporal and fading, Christ's kingdom is eternal, "Thy throne, O God, is forever and ever," (Psalm 45:6).

When Scripture says that the dominion under the whole heaven will be given to the saints and that the kingdoms of the earth will become Christ's, it does not mean that His kingdom will cease to be spiritual or that the kingdoms of the world will lose their natural characteristics. Instead, these earthly kingdoms will come under the influence and guidance of Christ's rule through His people. This change will be as transformative as the conversion of a sinner, who remains the same person in nature but is made a "new creature" in Christ (2 Corinthians 5:17). The kingdoms of the world will continue to function on principles of natural justice, but they will be governed by saints who act in accordance with Christ's laws.

This does not disrupt natural governance but perfects it. The influence of Christ's kingdom on earthly rule will result in justice, peace, and righteousness. As Psalm 97:1 declares, "The LORD reigneth; let the earth rejoice." When saints govern, they will do so as stewards of Christ, maintaining justice and righteousness while acting as subjects of His spiritual kingdom. The world will have no cause to fear the reign of such rulers, for they will act in obedience to Christ's commands, ensuring their rule benefits all. As Psalm 47:1 proclaims: "O clap your hands, all ye people; shout unto God with the voice of triumph." The people of the earth will rejoice in that day when the kingdoms of this world are brought under the righteous and gracious dominion of Christ through His saints.

I now proceed to the application of this doctrine, focusing primarily on two points. First, I will address how it relates to the doctrine of *Infant Baptism*. Second, I will discuss its *implications* for the Kingdom of Christ. Concerning Infant Baptism, I will not explore deeply the broader controversy but will restrict myself to arguments arising from this particular teaching. While other arguments are valid and relevant, I will not address them here. To frame the discussion, let us consider key insights derived from the explanation of this doctrine.

Use 1. From this teaching, we can observe the similarities and differences between the two great promises made by God to His people. The first is the promise given to our first parents in Genesis 3:15: "The seed of the woman shall bruise the serpent's head." The second is the promise made to Abraha, "Blessing I will bless thee, and thou shalt be a blessing; and in thee shall all the families of the earth be blessed. And multiplying I will multiply thy seed," and so forth. These promises are alike in several ways:

1. Both are fulfilled in Christ.

2. Both are given to a spiritual seed.

3. Both aim to increase that seed and ensure victory over enemies.

4. Both encompass the entirety of the Gospel.

However, they differ in that the promise to Abraham adds specific details regarding how this conquest will be accomplished:

1. By establishing the spiritual seed as a kingdom. Previously, God's people existed in families, but now many families are joined together as a distinct, holy nation and *kingdom*. As Exodus 19:6 declares, "Ye shall be unto me a kingdom of priests and an holy nation." This kingdom began with Abraham when God chose his seed. It was carried on in the Church of the Old Testament and continues in the Church of the New Testament, though administered differently. Yet, it remains the same kingdom, as Christ Himself said, "The kingdom of God shall be taken from you [*the Jews*] and given to a nation bringing forth the fruits thereof," (Matthew 21:43). This kingdom, in essence, existed from the beginning, but its formal establishment and the inheritance of the world through Abraham's seed began with God's promise to Abraham.

2. By appointing a means for the kingdom's growth and greatness, God blesses believers so they may become blessings to families, kindreds, and nations, thereby multiplying the *spiritual* seed. As discussed earlier, this involves God's ordinary work of placing elect children with elect parents.

This brings us to another significant addition, the introduction of circumcision as a seal of the covenant, first given to Abraham. Circumcision was not previously in use. This seal corresponded to the added promise of believers being blessings to families and nations and served to signify and confirm that promise. As Genesis 17:10 declares, "This is my covenant, which ye shall keep, between me and you and thy seed after thee: every man-child among you shall be circumcised." Moreover, the warning is added in verse 14,

"The uncircumcised man-child... shall be cut off from his people; he hath broken my covenant." This shows that applying the seal to infants was integral to the covenant. If it had not been part of the covenant, the omission of circumcision for infants would not have been a breach.

Further evidence comes from Acts 7:8: "He gave him the covenant of circumcision, and so Abraham begat Isaac and circumcised him the eighth day." Abraham circumcised Isaac as required by the covenant of circumcision, which mandated that the seal be applied to infants as part of the covenantal obligation. This confirms that the application of the seal to infants symbolized and affirmed God's promise to bless families and posterity.

This point is further reinforced by Deuteronomy 30:6: "And the LORD thy God will circumcise thine heart, and the heart of thy seed." This promise connects circumcision with the spiritual blessing of conversion for believers' children. Just as baptism signifies union with Christ (1 Corinthians 12:13), circumcision signified the promise of heart transformation for the children of God's covenant people.

Had the application of circumcision to infants been omitted, the sign would not have matched the promise, which included blessings for posterity. Since this blessing on families and posterity is a unique feature of God's covenant with Abraham—absent from the covenant with Adam—its omission from the seal would have been incongruent. The application of the seal to infants aligns with God's design to signify and confirm the promise to families and posterity.

In this way, denying this privilege to infants is a rejection of what God *granted* in Abraham's covenant. Genesis 17 warns, "The uncircumcised man-child... shall be cut off from his people; he hath broken my covenant."

It is also worth noting that Abraham's designation as, "the father of all them that believe," (Romans 4:11) is tied to these two features: the additional promise *and its seal*.

First, the additional promise made him the father of many nations. Romans 4:18 states, "Who against hope believed in hope, that he might become the father of many nations, according to that which was spoken, So shall thy seed be," referring to Genesis 15:5. It was Abraham's specific belief in this promise of multiplied seed that made him the father of many nations.

Second, this title also derives from his receiving the seal of that promise. Romans 4:11 states, "He received the sign of circumcision, a seal of the righteousness of the faith which he had being yet uncircumcised, that he might be the father of all them that believe." Circumcision was given to confirm his status as the father of believers, regardless of whether they were circumcised or uncircumcised. Thus, this seal was essential in establishing his universal spiritual fatherhood.

The argument begins with examining why Abraham was called, "the father of the faithful," and it is established that this title was not given merely because of his faith or the degree of his faith.

Reasons for Abraham's Designation. 1. Faith Alone was insufficient. If faith alone were the basis, Eve could be called, "the mother of the faithful," or Adam "the father," since they were the first believers. Others like Enoch and Noah likely had faith as strong as Abraham's. In Hebrews 11, where many heroes of faith are commended, Abraham's faith is not ranked above theirs. Moreover, Melchizedek is described in Hebrews 7 as greater than Abraham in one respect, "He blessed Abraham, and without all contradiction the less is blessed of the better," (Hebrews 7:7). The distinction given to Abraham was not based on the strength of his faith but *on the unique promises* he received as the father of believers.

2. A New Revelation Was Given to Abraham. When God changed Abram's name to *Abraham* and made him, "the father of the faithful," He revealed something new. Just as Peter's new name symbolized the keys to the kingdom, and Jacob's new name "Israel" represented his prevailing with God in prayer, so Abraham's new name pointed to his unique role. God began His kingdom in Abraham, establishing a peculiar people for Himself. Though Esau and Ishmael opposed this kingdom in different ways, Esau was the first to seek its destruction outright, forcing Jacob to rely on God's promise. Abraham's title reflects a new covenantal blessing—one not granted to believers before him.

3. The Name Was Given for a Specific Purpose. The name Abraham, meaning ,"Father of Multitudes," was given because of the promise that he would become the father of many nations: "Thy name shall be Abraham; for a father of many nations have I made thee," (Genesis 17:5). This promise was fulfilled in the additional covenant blessing that believers, as Abraham's spiritual seed, would propagate

and multiply through families and nations. His designation as, "father of the faithful" reflects not only his role as the first recipient of this blessing but also as the one through whom God's promise of spiritual multiplication would be carried out.

4. Believers are His Seed Not Solely by Faithful Example. While believers are said to, "walk in the steps of the faith of Abraham," (Romans 4:12), this is not the sole reason they are called his seed. Hebrews 12:1 urges believers to consider the examples of many faithful witnesses, not just Abraham, and especially Christ. Abraham's title is tied to God's promise to multiply his spiritual seed through blessings upon families and nations.

Application of Infant Baptism. The doctrine of *Infant Baptism* is supported by considering the covenant with Abraham and the addition made to the promise given to Adam. From this covenant, five observations are made:

1. An Additional Promise Was Given to Abraham. The covenant with Abraham expanded the promise given to Adam, introducing blessings upon families and nations to multiply the spiritual seed.

2. A Seal Was Added. Circumcision was introduced as the covenant seal, a new sign accompanying this expanded promise.

3. The Application of the Seal to Infants. The inclusion of infants in circumcision was a *fundamental* part of *the covenant*. The child's failure to receive circumcision was considered a breach of the covenant (Genesis 17:14). This application signified blessings for families and posterity.

4. The Seal Confirmed the Promise of Multiplication. The application of circumcision to infants sealed the promise of multiplying the seed through blessings on families and nations.

5. Abraham as the Father of Believers. Abraham was designated, "the father of the faithful," in reference to this additional promise and its seal. His reception of the covenant and its sign was not for himself alone but for his spiritual seed in their generations.

Consolation for Believers. The second application draws from the Apostle's conclusion in Hebrews 6:17-18, where God's oath to Abraham provides believers with, "strong consolation." This covenant and promise are designed to strengthen the faith and hope of believers, calling them to rejoice in the heavenly realities symbolized by the promises. Faith enables them to rest confidently in God's immutability and His eternal blessings.

Believers should not neglect the covenantal privileges God has extended to them and their children. These blessings, which have provided joy and assurance to the saints throughout history, should not be lightly set aside. Parents are exhorted to remember their responsibility to their children, ensuring they are not excluded from Christ's kingdom. Children will belong to either the kingdom of Christ or the kingdom of Satan, and believers should earnestly labor to bring them under the blessings of the covenant.

Covenantal Responsibilities. Finally, as the covenant with Abraham involves duties as well as promises, believers are called to search out and fulfill their obligations.

God's covenant is both a privilege and a command, requiring believers to walk faithfully in obedience to their covenantal responsibilities.

Application 3. This section leads us to understand that the great promise made to Abraham and his seed in Genesis 17 should not be confined merely to the earthly land of Canaan, nor should it be interpreted solely as pertaining to temporal blessings or the multiplication of Abraham's natural descendants in that land. Rather, it also encompasses *spiritual blessings in Christ*, of which the earthly Canaan and its benefits were *types* and *shadows*. The promise in Genesis 17:8, stating that the land of Canaan would be an everlasting possession for Abraham's seed and that God would be their God, is still being fulfilled *to believers in the New Testament era* through the spiritual blessings of the heavenly Canaan and the conquest of the world by the people of the God of Abraham. This fulfillment mirrors the conquest of the earthly Canaan by Joshua, which served as a type.

If someone argues that this promise cannot extend to these times in either of these two ways, such a person must propose another interpretation that allows the promise to extend to the present, as the Lord's confirmation to Abraham—of blessing, multiplying, and enabling his seed to possess the gates of their enemies—is explicitly confirmed to believers in the New Testament as Abraham's spiritual seed and heirs according to the promise.

In explaining this point, we have already provided extensive proof and have addressed related aspects of the Kingdom of Christ. While a full exposition of that kingdom requires a larger discussion, its relation to infant baptism helps clarify how the promise made to Abraham, which includes blessing and multiplying his seed, establishes duties for believers today.

Infant Baptism and the Covenant with Abraham. If it is acknowledged that the promise made to Abraham in Genesis 17, particularly verse 8 regarding Canaan as an everlasting possession for his seed, extends to his spiritual seed in the New Testament, then it follows that the command in verse 9— "Thou shalt keep my covenant therefore, thou and thy seed after thee, in their generations"—applies equally to his spiritual seed now, throughout all generations. This command is presented as a direct consequence of the promise, as indicated by the word "therefore."

The command continues in verse 10, "This is my covenant, which ye shall keep, between me and you and thy seed after thee; every man child among you shall be circumcised. And ye shall circumcise the flesh of your foreskin; and it shall be a token of the covenant betwixt me and you," and verse 14 adds, "The uncircumcised man child... hath broken my covenant."

Objection. It may be objected that since circumcision is now abolished, the command of keeping this covenant no longer applies to believers. Additionally, it might be questioned how this relates to baptizing children, the issue under discussion.

Answer. 1. The Command Is General. The command primarily requires the covenant to be kept in general, not through any specific sign, such as circumcision. Circumcision was included under the command only because it was then designated as the token of the covenant. However, the language implies that when circumcision ceased to be the covenant's token, it would no longer be obligatory. Whatever else God appointed as the token of the same covenant would take its place as the duty to be observed.

The command does not explicitly state, "Thou shalt therefore circumcise every man child," as if circumcision were the perpetual token of the covenant. Instead, it says, "Thou shalt keep my covenant therefore, thou and thy seed after thee, in their generations." This language emphasizes the *general* obligation to keep the covenant, regardless of the specific sign associated with it.

2. Change in the Covenant's Token. Circumcision is abolished, yet the command to observe the token of Abraham's covenant *remains binding* upon Abraham's spiritual seed across generations. Therefore, the current token of the covenant, baptism, must be observed in its place.

3. Parallel with the Sabbath. The institution of the Sabbath provides a helpful comparison. God intended to change the Sabbath day from the seventh day to the first day of the week, just as He intended to change the token of Abraham's covenant. In the Fourth Commandment, the obligation is not primarily tied to the seventh day but to the principle of keeping the rest-day holy, regardless of which day is designated. The command says, "Remember the Sabbath day, to keep it holy," without permanently fixing it to the seventh day.

Initially, the seventh day was sanctified because it commemorated God's rest after creation. When Christ completed His redemptive work, entering into His rest on the first day of the week through His resurrection, the Sabbath shifted to that day. Hebrews 4:9-10 affirms this new rest, as does Mark 2:28, where Christ declares Himself, "Lord also of the Sabbath." By the same principle, the command to keep Abraham's covenant applies to its current token, baptism, which has replaced circumcision.

This argument establishes that the promise made to Abraham in Genesis 17 is still valid for believers today and includes the obligation to keep the covenant in its current form. As circumcision was the token under the Old Testament, baptism now serves as the *corresponding token* under the New Testament. The general obligation to observe the covenant remains binding upon Abraham's spiritual seed in all generations, making infant baptism a duty required by God's command.

The ascension of Christ is not as clearly evidenced to have occurred on the first day of the week as His resurrection, though it is probable, based on Acts 1. The computation of forty days from His resurrection, along with the reference to, "a Sabbath day's journey" from Mount Olivet to Jerusalem, suggests that the disciples made that journey on the first day (Acts 1:12). Although Christ's rest was not fully completed until He ascended into heaven and sat at the right hand of the Majesty on high, He first entered into His rest at His resurrection, for He was raised incorruptible, with a spiritual body, and in glory (1 Corinthians 15:42–43, 49, 20). At that moment, He ceased from the travail of His soul. Since this occurred on the first day of the week, it sufficiently establishes this day as the one God sanctified and blessed. This falls under the general rule that the Lord's rest day must be remembered and kept holy, for the Lord blessed the rest day and sanctified it.

To analyze the fourth commandment regarding the Sabbath, we may understand it as follows:

1. A Duty Commanded. The command is to remember the Lord's rest day, that is, the day He entered into His rest, by observing its memorial and keeping it holy. The word "remember" in this context signifies preserving the memorial of the day by *solemn observation*. This usage is consistent with Exodus 13:3–9, where Moses commands the Israelites to, "remember this day, in which ye came out from Egypt," and Esther 9:27–28, where the Jews ordained that the days of Purim "should be remembered, and kept throughout every generation."

2. Explanation of the Duty.

The Day. In General: One day in seven is set aside. "Six days shalt thou labor, and do all thy work," (Exodus 20:9). In Particular: At that time, the seventh day of the week was designated. "The seventh day is the Sabbath of the Lord thy God," (Exodus 20:10).

The Manner of Observing It: Complete rest from labor is required. "Thou shalt not do any work, thou, nor thy son, nor thy daughter, thy manservant, nor thy maidservant, nor thy cattle, nor thy stranger that is within thy gates," (Exodus 20:10). This prohibition encompasses all other duties appropriate to the Sabbath by a synecdoche.

3. The Reason for the Duty. God created the world in six days and rested on the seventh. He blessed the rest day and sanctified it because He rested on it. From this analysis, we see that the seventh day was commanded to be observed, not because it was the seventh day *specifically*, but because it was the Lord's rest day. The reason for the command lies in the fact that God rested on that day and therefore blessed and sanctified it. This explanation concerning the Sabbath bears a resemblance to the discussion of infant baptism, as both are often disputed. Understanding the Sabbath helps illuminate the matter of Abraham's covenant. In Abraham's covenant, as in the fourth commandment, we find:

1. A Duty Commanded: To keep the covenant, including its token, sign, or seal. Abraham and his seed were required to observe this.

2. An Explanation: The token at that time was circumcision, and failure to observe it was a breach of the covenant (Genesis 17:10, 14).

In this way, even though circumcision as a token is now abolished, the command to keep the covenant by observing its token remains in force for Abraham's spiritual seed today.

Baptism as the Token of the Covenant. Baptism has replaced circumcision as the token and seal of the covenant. This is evident in Galatians 3:27–29, "As many of you as have been baptized into Christ have put on Christ. And if ye be Christ's, then are ye Abraham's seed, and heirs according to the promise." All that we have as Abraham's seed, we have in Christ, and all that we have in Christ, we have as Abraham's seed. Baptism seals this relationship with Christ and the inheritance of Abraham's promise. Thus, baptism serves the same purpose for believers today as circumcision did for Abraham's descendants. Further confirmation is found in Colossians 2:11–12: "In whom also ye are circumcised with the circumcision made without hands, in putting off the body of the sins of the flesh by the circumcision of Christ, buried with him in baptism, wherein also ye are risen with him." This passage demonstrates that:

1. The spiritual fruit of circumcision, the putting off of sin, is also the fruit of baptism, which signifies death and resurrection to a new life in Christ.

2. Those who are in Christ partake of this circumcision of the heart, which Christ accomplished for His people.

3. Baptism conveys the same spiritual benefit, signifying burial with Christ and resurrection in Him.

In this way, the benefits of circumcision—spiritual renewal and participation in Christ—are now signified and sealed in baptism. The Apostle Paul *explicitly* links the two, showing that baptism now occupies the same role as circumcision did, sealing the covenant for Abraham's seed.

Abraham received the sign of circumcision as the father of all who believe, not only for himself but for his seed, both Jews and Gentiles. Baptism now serves the same purpose, sealing the covenant for Abraham's spiritual descendants. This continuity between circumcision and baptism underscores the enduring nature of the covenant and its application to Abraham's seed across generations. Genesis 17:9–10 confirms this command, "Thou shalt keep my covenant therefore, thou and thy seed after thee in their generations. This is my covenant, which ye shall keep, between me and you and thy seed after thee; Every man child among you shall be circumcised." Thus, the principle remains, though the outward token has changed.

It should not be overlooked, as further evidence that baptism has replaced circumcision, that the Lord's Supper is, for substance, the same as the Passover. This is evident from 1 Corinthians 5:7–8: "Purge out therefore the old leaven, that ye may be a new lump, as ye are unleavened. For even Christ our passover is sacrificed for us, therefore let us keep the feast, not with old leaven, neither with the leaven of malice and wickedness; but with the unleavened bread of sincerity and truth." The Apostle speaks this in the context of the Church purging out the wicked person among them, as he explains in verse 13. This person, like leaven, had corrupted the congregation, which Paul likens to a single loaf of bread when celebrating the Lord's Supper (1 Corinthians 10:17). The Apostle's use of language from the Passover, particularly regarding unleavened bread, would not make sense unless the Passover and the Lord's Supper were *substantially* the same.

Objection. If it is granted that baptism is, for substance, the same as circumcision and has replaced it as the seal of the same covenant made with Abraham, and if it is accepted that Abraham's seed is still bound to observe the token of this covenant in all generations, how does this prove that infants should be baptized? Can baptism not remain the seal of Abraham's covenant while being administered only to those of mature age who can confess their faith?

Response. First, consider what was demonstrated in the earlier argument: the application of the seal to infants is a part of the covenant itself. This application is an essential aspect of the token of the covenant. Without it, the covenant is *not* fully kept, nor is God's command fulfilled: "Thou shalt keep my covenant therefore, thou and thy seed after thee in their generations," (Genesis 17:9). If the seal is withheld from infants, the covenant is broken, as stated in Genesis 17:14: "The uncircumcised man-child... hath broken my covenant." The reason for this is that the application of the seal to infants signified and confirmed the branch of the covenant uniquely *given to Abraham*—a blessing upon his descendants. Removing this application would nullify a key feature of Abraham's covenant, reducing it to the form of prior covenants and effectively breaking it. If this blessing upon posterity remains in effect under the New Testament, then the application of the seal to infants, which signified and confirmed that blessing, must also remain.

Second, even if the application of the seal to infants were considered a mere circumstance rather than an essential aspect of the covenant, no change in that circumstance can be made without an explicit word from the Lord. For example, the shift from circumcision to baptism as the token of the covenant is supported by clear divine instruction. Similarly, the inclusion of females under the seal of the covenant in the New Testament is warranted by Acts 8:12, where it is noted that both men and women were baptized when they believed the preaching of Philip. This inclusion is further explained in Galatians 3:27–28, which declares that, "as many of you as have been baptized into Christ have put on Christ. There is neither Jew nor Greek, there is neither bond nor free, there is neither male nor female: for ye are all one in Christ Jesus." Under the law, distinctions of privilege existed: Jews over Greeks, males over females. But in Christ, these distinctions are removed. Therefore, the seal of Abraham's covenant is now applied to females as well as males. If any seek to alter the application further, such as by excluding infants, they must provide *explicit divine warrant* for doing so.

Third, those who oppose infant baptism often claim they are merely withholding a practice for which there is no command or example in Scripture. They demand proof of a specific precept or precedent for baptizing infants and consider its absence sufficient grounds to reject the practice. This reasoning is mistaken. The command is clear in Genesis 17:9: "Thou shalt keep my covenant therefore, thou and thy seed after thee in their generations." As previously shown, this command applies to Abraham's spiritual seed under the New Testament. Those who deny infant baptism must demonstrate that God has explicitly altered this covenant's token, removing its application to infants. They must show that what was once an essential aspect of the covenant has now ceased to be so by divine institution.

Lastly, the application of the seal to infants is not only a duty but also a privilege. Acts 7:8 states, "He gave him the covenant of circumcision: and so Abraham begat Isaac, and circumcised him the eighth day." This was a gift from God, conferred upon Abraham and his descendants. Since it was given to Abraham and his spiritual seed across generations as a privilege for both parents and children, it cannot be taken away without clear authorization from God. Romans 11:29 declares that, "the gifts and calling of God are without repentance." Therefore, it cannot be imagined that God would *withdraw* this privilege in the New Testament era, especially when His grace toward His people has only abounded more fully.

It may further be objected that the command regarding the application of the token of Abraham's covenant to infants, as urged from Genesis 17, comes only from the Old Testament. If such an application were intended to continue under the New Testament, surely the New Testament would not be silent on the matter, leaving us without even one precept or example to confirm it.

Response. First Answer. The New Testament is not entirely silent on this issue. Consider Acts 2:38–39, where Peter said to the people, "Repent, and be baptized every one of you in the name of Jesus Christ for the remission of sins, and ye shall receive the gift of the Holy Ghost. For the promise is unto you, and to your children, and to all that are afar off, even as many as the Lord our God shall call." The promise of receiving the Holy Ghost, which Peter connects to repentance and baptism, fulfills the prophecy in Joel 2:28–29, mentioned earlier in the chapter (Acts 2:17). Joel foretold that, "in the last days" God would pour out His Spirit upon all flesh—on Gentiles as well as Jews. This promise also aligns with the covenant God made with Abraham, as Paul explains in Galatians 3:13–14, "Christ hath redeemed us from the curse of the law, being made a curse for us... that the blessing of Abraham might come on the

Gentiles through Jesus Christ; that we might receive the promise of the Spirit through faith."

This promise in Joel cannot be confined merely to extraordinary gifts, such as tongues or miracles, because it extends beyond the Apostolic age into the latter days. The phrase "last days" in Scripture refers to the entire period from Christ's incarnation to the end of the world, as shown in 1 Timothy 4:1, 2 Timothy 3:1, Hebrews 1:2, and Hebrews 9:26. Additionally, the words of Joel's prophecy include ordinary gifts of the Spirit, not only miraculous ones.

Joel states, "I will pour out my Spirit upon all flesh," which broadly refers to *all* believers. He continues, "Your sons and your daughters shall prophesy, your young men shall see visions, your old men shall dream dreams." These extraordinary gifts applied to the Apostles and other early Church leaders for laying the foundations of the New Testament Church. However, Joel also says, "And on my servants and on my handmaids I will pour out in those days of my Spirit, and they shall prophesy," which refers to ordinary gifts shared by all believers. Revelation 19:10 defines the "spirit of prophecy" as "the testimony of Jesus," a gift every believer possesses, "The dragon was wroth with the woman, and went to make war with the remnant of her seed, which keep the commandments of God, and have the testimony of Jesus Christ," (Revelation 12:17). Even those described as "little children" in faith are said to possess this testimony (1 John 2:20, 27).

Through Christ's death and resurrection, believers now receive the Spirit in greater measure, enabling them to understand what was previously hidden (Revelation 5).

Therefore, the promise of the Spirit's outpouring includes ordinary gifts, empowering believers to discern truth and grow in faith, just as Joel and Peter affirmed.

Second Answer. In Acts 2, Peter extends the invitation to repentance and baptism to the Jews and their children, affirming their continued inclusion in the covenant. However, the promise does not belong to them merely as Abraham's natural descendants but as believers, because they have embraced repentance and faith. This is evident for three reasons:

1. What belonged to the Jews as Abraham's natural descendants was circumcision, not baptism.

2. John the Baptist made this clear when he rebuked those who relied on their physical descent from Abraham. He said, "Bring forth therefore fruits worthy of repentance, and begin not to say within yourselves, We have Abraham to our father," (Luke 3:8).

3. Peter applies the same promise to Gentiles, stating it belongs to as many of them, "as the Lord our God shall call." This call implies faith and repentance, which are necessary for participation in the covenant.

Therefore, Peter speaks to the crowd of repentant Jews who had believed in Christ and assures them that the promise of the Spirit is not only for them but also for their children and the Gentiles who come to faith. This declaration comforts them by confirming that their sins—even their rejection and crucifixion of Christ—will not exclude them from the blessings of the covenant if they repent. Likewise, it shows that the promise of Abraham's covenant, including its application to children, continues under the New Testament for all who believe.

This passage clarifies further the understanding of how the covenant with Abraham, particularly its application to infants through circumcision, continues to inform New Testament practices, including baptism, as a sign and seal of the same covenant.

Addressing the Objection. Objection: It may be argued that the New Testament does not provide sufficient explicit evidence for the continuation of applying the covenant's token to children, leaving this as an Old Testament command with no direct instruction in the New Testament.

Answer: 1. Peter's Declaration in Acts 2:38–39. Peter's words affirm the continuity of the covenant: "Repent, and be baptized every one of you in the name of Jesus Christ for the remission of sins, and ye shall receive the gift of the Holy Ghost. For the promise is unto you, and to your children, and to all that are afar off, even as many as the Lord our God shall call." This statement confirms that the promise extends not only to the Jewish hearers but also to their children, consistent with the covenantal structure established with Abraham. The promise also applies to Gentiles ("to all that are afar off") when they, too, are effectually called by God.

In interpreting this passage, note that Scripture often uses a structure in which the meaning of one part of a sentence is clarified or expanded by the other. For example, Psalm 1:6 states, "The Lord knoweth the way of the righteous: but the way of the ungodly shall perish," implying that the way of the ungodly is unknown to the Lord in the sense of approval, just as the way of the righteous will not perish. Similarly, Proverbs 10:24 states, "The fear of the wicked, it shall come upon him, but the desire of the righteous shall be granted," implying the converse—that the desires of the wicked will not be granted, and the righteous will be delivered from fear.

Applying this reasoning to Acts 2:39, when Peter says, "The promise is unto you, and to your children, and to all that are afar off, even as many as the Lord our God shall call," it follows that the promise includes both Jews and Gentiles who are effectually called, along with their children. The promise of the Holy Spirit, tied to the covenant, in this way extends to children in the same way it did under Abraham's covenant, even if not explicitly repeated in every instance.

2. The Old and New Testament Unity in the Covenant. The ordinances of worship are only briefly mentioned in the New Testament because they *assume* the foundation laid in the Old Testament. The Old Testament served as the season of instruction in the Law, while the New Testament emphasizes the fuller revelation of the Gospel. Luke 16:16 affirms this distinction: "The law and the prophets were until John, since that time the kingdom of God is preached." This does not imply that the Gospel began with John or that the Law ended, but rather that the season of Gospel revelation had come, with the Law's principles continuing alongside it.

Psalm 78:1–8 provides further evidence. This psalm, a prophecy fulfilled in Christ (as shown in Matthew 13:35), presents Christ teaching his disciples God's Law through the history of Israel's provocations and God's dealings with them. This instruction applies to future generations, even in the New Testament era. Verse 5 states, "He established a testimony in Jacob, and appointed a law in Israel, which he commanded our fathers, that they should make them known to their children," showing the continuity of the Law across generations.

3. The Law and Gospel as One Unified Revelation. While the particular circumstances and duties of the Law may differ between the Testaments, the substance remains the same. Both convey a rule of service to God and include spiritual ordinances tied to blessings and penalties. For example, Hebrews 9 acknowledges that both the Old and New Covenants include ordinances of divine worship. Romans 7:12 affirms, "The law is holy, and the commandment holy, and just, and good." Even moral duties, now aimed at a spiritual end, are united with the new ordinances instituted in Christ.

The Apostle Paul's warnings in 1 Corinthians 10 illustrate this unity. The Israelites experienced spiritual realities in their wilderness journey, "They were all baptized unto Moses in the cloud and in the sea; and did all eat the same spiritual meat; and did all drink the same spiritual drink," (1 Corinthians 10:2-4). Yet, they fell into sin and faced judgment, which Paul applies to New Testament believers, "All these things happened unto them for ensamples, and they are written for our admonition, upon whom the ends of the world are come," (1 Corinthians 10:11).

Similarly, Psalm 95, applied by the author of Hebrews, warns believers not to provoke God as the Israelites did in the wilderness, emphasizing the continued relevance of these lessons under the New Covenant.

Application to Infant Baptism. These principles affirm that the application of the covenant's token to children, integral to the covenant with Abraham, has not been abrogated. The general structure of God's covenant with His people—His promises to believers and their children—continues unchanged. The New Testament does not nullify this aspect but builds upon it, assuming the Church's understanding of its Old Testament foundations. As circumcision was administered to infants under Abraham's covenant, so baptism, as the covenant's seal under the New Testament, naturally extends to children of believers unless expressly revoked, which the Scriptures nowhere indicate.

The text asserts that the covenant established with Abraham, including the application of its seal to infants, remains relevant under the New Testament administration and is integral to the covenant of grace. It directly responds to objections about the absence of explicit references to infant baptism in the New Testament by emphasizing continuity with Old Testament teachings.

It begins by *rejecting* the notion that the covenant with Abraham or the Law in the Old Testament constitutes a covenant of works for New Testament believers. While the Law was initially given to Adam in a covenant of works, it has, since the Fall, *been integrated into the covenant of grace*. This is evident because the Law, as delivered by Moses, is considered part of *Christ's* covenant, confirmed by His blood. As Hebrews 9:16–18 explains, even the first covenant was not ratified without blood, symbolized by sacrifices under the Old Testament and fulfilled in Christ's own sacrifice. Therefore, the Law given by Moses is not a standalone covenant of works but part of the overarching covenant of grace.

The text references Deuteronomy 30:12–14, where Moses explains that God's word is not far off or inaccessible but is "very nigh unto thee, in thy mouth, and in thy heart," which Paul in Romans 10:6 applies to the Gospel. This demonstrates the unity of God's covenant across both Testaments, showing that the Law, when viewed apart from grace, could appear as a covenant of works but has always functioned as part of the covenant of grace since the Fall.

Christ's role as the head of His kingdom transforms the Law's application. Under the covenant of grace:

1. The Law is kept through Christ's strength: In the covenant of works, the command was "Do this and live." Under the covenant of grace, it is "Do this in the strength of Christ and live."

2. State and condition depend on grace: A believer's standing before God is based on Christ's merits, not their own adherence to the Law. While obedience affects comfort and blessings, it does not determine eternal standing.

3. Freedom from the Law's eternal curse: Believers are no longer subject to the eternal condemnation of the Law. Christ's justice, as a loving Father, aims at correction and restoration, not destruction.

4. Punishments under Christ's justice are redemptive: When Christ disciplines His followers, He does so as a Father aiming for their good, not simply as a judge executing justice.

This understanding of the covenant helps address the objection that infant baptism lacks explicit mention in the New Testament. The author emphasizes that the New Testament often assumes knowledge of Old Testament teachings, particularly concerning the Law and ordinances of worship, which were given in detail under the Old Testament. The Law and the prophets were a preparation, unfolding doctrines that the New Testament builds upon without reiterating every detail. Luke 16:16 states, "The law and the prophets were until John, since that time the kingdom of God is preached." This shows that while the Gospel was more fully revealed after John, the Law's teachings remain foundational.

Psalm 78 illustrates how the Old Testament served as an instructional foundation for all future generations. It recounts God's dealings with Israel, emphasizing His faithfulness and discipline, which were meant to teach future generations to trust and obey Him. This teaching continues under Christ's administration, as reflected in parables like the sower in Matthew 13, which parallel the lessons of Psalm 78. These examples demonstrate that the Law's substance and purpose remain relevant, even as some outward forms change.

The text then argues that the general nature of the Law is consistent across both Testaments. The Law provides a divinely prescribed method of service to God, consisting of spiritual ordinances meant to lead believers into communion with Him. The Sabbath commandment is cited as an example. Although the specific day has changed from the seventh to the first day of the week, the general command to remember and keep the rest day remains binding. This illustrates how changes in the outward administration of the Law do not alter its essence.

Finally, the text addresses the silence of the New Testament regarding infant baptism. This silence is presented as evidence *in favor of its continuation*, rather than against it. Since the Old Testament so clearly establishes the application of the covenant seal to infants, it would have been unnecessary for the New Testament to repeat what was already universally accepted. If the practice were to be discontinued, explicit instruction to that effect would have been necessary, especially considering the numerous questions and disputes addressed by the Apostles. The absence of such a prohibition implies that infant baptism was assumed as part of the covenant's continuity.

The text concludes by affirming that the covenant with Abraham, with its promise of blessings upon families and its application to infants, remains intact under the New Testament. The inclusion of infants in the covenant was integral to its administration and would not have been omitted without explicit divine instruction. Thus, the practice of infant baptism aligns with the covenantal framework established by God and faithfully continued through Christ.

The text explains why the Apostle Paul refers to the children of believing parents as "holy" in 1 Corinthians 7:14, contrasting them with those who are considered "common" or "unclean." This distinction is grounded in the covenantal blessings given to Abraham, which extend to believers and their children.

Paul's statement draws on the covenant promise: "Blessing I will bless thee, and thou shalt be a blessing, and in thee shall all the families of the earth be blessed," (Genesis 12:2-3). The blessings God confers are accompanied by sanctification and separation, as with the Sabbath, which God blessed and made holy by distinguishing it from common days. Similarly, the children of believers are set apart by God's blessing and are not to be regarded as merely under common providence, such as the blessings of nature and upbringing, which all creation enjoys.

The author illustrates this point by distinguishing between ordinary blessings and spiritual blessings. While all creation benefits from God's providence— "The earth which drinketh in the rain...receiveth blessing from God," (Hebrews 6:7)—this does not confer holiness. True holiness involves separation for a spiritual and supernatural purpose, as is the case with the children of believing parents. These children are under a specific divine blessing that includes the promise of their conversion to God. Without this divine blessing, even the best parental prayers, examples, and education would lack spiritual efficacy.

Paul further distinguishes between Jews and Gentiles using the metaphor of the olive tree in Romans 11:24. The Jews are described as the "natural branches" of the good olive tree, and the Gentiles as branches from a wild olive tree grafted in. This difference is not rooted in nature, as both Jews and Gentiles are equally born in sin, but in God's covenantal grace. The Jews were given the means of grace and God's covenantal promises, while the Gentiles were left without such means, growing wild under God's curse. This distinction explains why the children of believing parents are "holy" in a covenantal sense, set apart under the blessings of God's promises.

The text acknowledges that while one cannot affirm with certainty that any particular infant of believing parents is inherently holy, they are holy in the sense of being separated unto God and distinguished from those who are unclean or common. This is comparable to the way church members are regarded as holy through their outward profession of faith, even though their internal state may be uncertain. The covenant promise to Abraham, which extends to families, provides believers with a positive ground for hope concerning their children's salvation.

The application of baptism to infants is defended on the same principle. Just as adults are baptized based on their profession of faith, which may not always reflect genuine spiritual regeneration, infants of believers are baptized based on God's covenantal promise. The author argues that God's appointment of infants to receive the seal of the covenant further establishes their covenantal holiness. The seal of baptism, being holy, is properly applied only to those regarded as holy in this covenantal sense.

The text refutes an alternative interpretation of 1 Corinthians 7:14, which claims that the children's holiness refers merely to their legitimacy. This interpretation fails to address the question posed to Paul about the lawfulness of a believer remaining married to an unbelieving spouse. If Paul's argument were simply that their children were legitimate, it would not resolve the concern about spiritual contamination from an unbelieving spouse. Instead, Paul's reasoning hinges on the sanctifying influence of the believing spouse, which extends covenantal blessings to the children, distinguishing them as holy.

The Jewish context of the question is emphasized. Under the Law, Israelites were forbidden from marrying outside the covenant community, and such unions required separation, as seen in Ezra 10:11-12. The Corinthians, influenced by this tradition, questioned whether marriage to an unbeliever was lawful under the New Testament. Paul's response affirms that the unbelieving spouse is sanctified in the believing spouse, meaning the marriage is lawful and does not result in spiritual defilement. Consequently, their children are also regarded as holy, not unclean or excluded from covenant blessings. Paul argues that if the marriage were unlawful, the children would also be excluded, as was the case under the Old Testament law.

This reasoning demonstrates that the children of believers are covenantally holy, not because of inherent righteousness but because of God's covenantal blessing and promise. This covenantal holiness justifies their inclusion in the visible church and their reception of baptism as the seal of the covenant.

If it is objected that, based on this reasoning, not only the children of believers but entire nations must be considered holy because the promise states that believers shall be blessings to nations, I respond as follows:

The case is not the same. Children are directly under this word of blessing due to their relationship *within the family*, just as the people of God in the Church are directly under the blessing that, "the Lord commandeth out of Zion," (Psalm 133:3). Nations, on the other hand, are under this blessing only in a more remote sense, through the influence of the saints in their families and the Church. Thus, while the Church and the children of believing families are holy, it does not follow that the nation, as a whole, is holy.

Additionally, children are subject to their parents and under their authority. Therefore, when parents, in their sanctification and consecration to God, give themselves to Him in faith and obedience, they also implicitly dedicate their children to God. A believer, in giving themselves to God, gives to Him everything within their control. This cannot be said of entire nations.

If it is further objected that the Jewish people as a whole are called holy, even though they are currently unbelievers, as stated in Romans 11:16, "If the firstfruit be holy, the lump is also holy; and if the root be holy, so are the branches," and yet they have no right to baptism, then the holiness of the children mentioned in 1 Corinthians 7:14 cannot be an argument for infant baptism. The argument continues, suggesting that unbelieving Jews are also considered holy based on their connection to Abraham's covenant, and therefore holiness in this context cannot justify baptizing children.

To this, I reply: it is true that the two passages are related, and both have been cited earlier to affirm the covenant promise of a blessing upon the descendants of believers, intended to increase the number of believers. However, there is a key distinction between them. In 1 Corinthians 7:14, the Apostle speaks of specific individuals, declaring that they are holy. In Romans 11, he does not mean that the individual Jews who persist in unbelief, nor the entire Jewish nation at the time, are holy in any sense. On the contrary, it is explicitly stated that they are, "broken off" from the holy root, (Romans 11:20), "cast away," (verse 15), and "enemies," (verse 28). Therefore, they are unclean and profane, not holy.

The assertion in Romans 11 that the Jewish people are holy does not apply to every individual or the nation, as a whole in its entirety, but to the people of Israel insofar as some of them have believed or will eventually believe. It is common in Scripture to use a synecdoche, attributing to the whole what properly applies to a part. For example, Revelation 17:16 states, "The ten kings shall hate the whore and shall burn her flesh with fire," yet in Revelation 18:9, some of these same kings are said to lament her fall. Similarly, it is said of the thieves crucified with Christ that they "reviled him" (Matthew 27:44; Mark 15:32), but one of them rebuked the other and honored Christ, saying, "Lord, remember me when thou comest into thy kingdom," (Luke 23:39-42). Such expressions indicate the general category or type of individuals rather than every specific person within that category.

In this way, when Romans 11 refers to the Jewish people as holy, it is speaking of the nation in terms of those *who have believed* or *will believe*. The Apostle attributes holiness to the entire group because he is addressing the kind or category of people—the Jews—not each individual. In 1 Corinthians 7:14, however, Paul explicitly declares particular individuals—children of believers—to be holy. This distinction clarifies that Romans 11 and 1 Corinthians 7 are not contradictory.

Furthermore, if Romans 11:16 is taken as referring to future generations, it is consistent with the covenant promise made to Abraham, which was not limited to those alive at any single point but extended to *all posterity*. Thus, when the Apostle speaks of the lump as holy, he refers to the Jewish people in their entirety across successive generations, recognizing that some are holy through faith, even if others are cast away. This understanding aligns with the Apostle's description of the Jews as both "enemies" and "beloved for the fathers' sakes" (Romans 11:28), depending on whether he refers to the unbelieving or believing portion of the nation.

Given the difference between these two passages, the argument for infant baptism based on 1 Corinthians 7:14 remains valid, despite objections from Romans 11:16. In 1 Corinthians 7:14, the Apostle directly affirms the holiness of specific children, making it a strong and relevant basis for understanding the covenant relationship and the application of its seal through baptism.

The words of our Savior to His disciples in Mark 10— "Suffer little children to come unto me, and forbid them not, for of such is the kingdom of God"—carry weighty meaning. "Of such" does not merely refer to children as having certain qualifications, as has been explained earlier, but rather to the fact that the kingdom of God *includes* little children as well. There is a reason for this.

First, our Savior mentions the kingdom of God specifically in this context, rather than referring to the Church or His people, because this kingdom is the one *initiated with Abraham*. Its greatness is rooted in the promise made to him of blessings upon families and posterity. Therefore, the children of believers are considered part of this kingdom. When believers bring their children to Christ, as those in Mark 10 did, it fulfills, in part, the promise made to Abraham. This act is one of the means ordained by God for the growth and expansion of Christ's kingdom.

Second, our Savior's command to permit little children to come to Him is grounded in the fact that they belong to the kingdom and that the promises of the kingdom extend to them. Since the gospel of the kingdom includes the promise that believers will be blessings to their children, leading to their conversion, it is appropriate and necessary for believers to bring their children to Christ in outward and visible ways. In Mark 10, this was done by bringing them to Christ so He could lay His hands on them and bless them. Similarly, in our time, baptism serves as an outward means of bringing children to Christ for His blessing.

Third, our Savior's displeasure and indignation with the disciples for rebuking those who, brought the children show the *significance* of this matter. The word used, denoting indignation, expresses the depth of *His anger*, comparable to the disciples' displeasure with James and John for seeking positions of prominence in the kingdom (Matthew 20:24). Christ's anger was stirred not only by His love for the parents and children but also by His own interest in the matter. His kingdom, the object of His divine purpose from the beginning, depends in part on little ones being brought to Him. By forbidding infants from coming to Him, the disciples opposed His kingdom's growth and His design. Let all disciples of Christ take care not to provoke His anger in this way.

From this, we can draw several conclusions relevant to the question of infant baptism. First, if infants are part of the kingdom of God, and the blessings of that kingdom belong to them, it follows, as Peter argued in Acts 10:47, that none can forbid baptism to those who are already part of the kingdom. Baptism is the seal of our entrance into the kingdom and its blessings. If infants are part of the kingdom, they are entitled to receive this seal as well.

Second, the command of Christ to allow children to come to Him is not limited to the time of His earthly ministry. It was recorded after His ascension and remains a perpetual obligation for all His disciples. These things were written for our instruction, and there is no other outward way given for bringing children to Christ so that He might bless them except baptism. In baptism, we are initiated into the kingdom, and its blessings are sealed to us. Just as Christ laid His hands on the children and blessed them, so in baptism, He still confers blessings upon them. Though infants cannot comprehend these outward signs, they are no less capable of receiving the blessings signified by them, for Christ Himself fulfills His part in the sacrament.

Third, to whom Christ is a King, He is also a Prophet. Therefore, as infants are part of His kingdom, they are also among His disciples. When the parents are converted, their children are placed in the path of the Spirit's teaching. Acts 15:10 refers to circumcision as, "a yoke put upon the neck of the disciples," showing that even children were included among the disciples under the Old Covenant. This addresses the objection from Matthew 28:19, where some argue that baptism is only for those who are made disciples through explicit profession of faith. While further discussion could be had regarding the interpretation of this passage, it is sufficient to note that the command to "baptize them" in Matthew 28:19 includes, by a synecdoche, all aspects of entering into the worship and ordinances of the gospel. Among these ordinances, the application of the token of Abraham's covenant to infants is included.

While this subject could be pursued further, it suffices to note that the inclusion of infants in the kingdom and their right to the seal of the covenant is a continuation of God's promise to Abraham. This promise, as well as the manner in which Christ's kingdom is to grow, provides ample evidence that children of believers are entitled to baptism, marking their entrance into the blessings of His kingdom.

This sixth point teaches us to correct misunderstandings about the Kingdom of God and to remove *prejudices* or *doubts* that may arise against it. Specifically, when the Scripture declares that, "the kingdom, and dominion, and the greatness of the kingdom under the whole heaven, shall be given to the people of the saints of the most High," and that "they shall fill the world, and the Lord shall subdue the people under them, and the nations under their feet," some may interpret these statements as harsh or even as justifications for believers to seek power through rebellion or disruption of civil peace. However, when rightly understood, these promises give no cause for such fears or suspicions.

First, as seen in the exposition of this point, while it is true that the Church of Christ is a growing entity—of which it is said, "of the increase of his government and peace there shall be no end"—and that the promise to Abraham's seed, of possessing the gates of their enemies, must be fulfilled in due time, God will bring about this growth and power in a natural, genuine, and righteous manner. God will accomplish this not by violence, for He expressly rejects such methods, saying, "They shall beat their swords into plowshares, and their spears into pruninghooks," (Isaiah 2:4). Instead, His kingdom grows by the word of truth, meekness, and righteousness (Psalm 45:4). The scepter of His kingdom is a righteous scepter, and there is no unrighteousness in it. This kingdom is spiritual and will remain so; when the Lord's mountain is exalted above the hills, it will *still be* the Lord's mountain. Its warfare is conducted with spiritual weapons, particularly the sword of the Spirit, which is the word of God. Through this word, wielded by His saints in their families and congregations, the Lord will make them blessings to one another. The kingdom will spread as leaven that gradually seasons the whole lump, ultimately filling the world with the knowledge of Christ. Such is the nature of the conquest by which His kingdom will be made great.

Second, note that this power, however it is expressed, will be given into the hands of Abraham's seed. The promise is specific: "Thy seed shall possess the gate of his enemies." This refers to Abraham's spiritual seed, including those of the New Testament, as has been demonstrated. It is not a promise to those who merely claim to be Abraham's seed but to those whom God will bless and multiply as His own. When this promise is fulfilled, it will be said, "The Lord reigneth; let the earth rejoice," (Psalm 97:1). This power, resting in the hands of the Lord's people, will not be a cause for grief but for joy.

It may be objected that hypocrites within the Church, though undiscovered, are considered Abraham's seed in the judgment of charity and are granted external privileges and ordinances accordingly. How then can this promise be restricted solely to the true spiritual seed of Abraham? While it is true that hypocrites are to be treated as Abraham's seed by the Church, there is a distinction between what the Church administers and what God bestows. This promise concerns what God will accomplish in His providence. He will cause the true seed of Abraham to possess the gate of their enemies. When the Scripture addresses the Church's responsibilities, it includes both good and bad branches of the vine. However, when it speaks of God's promises, these are confined to believers alone. Even external privileges, though dispensed by the Church to all its members, are granted by God only to true believers. Hypocrites partake of them at their own peril, while the Church faithfully administers its duty based on outward confession.

If the power of possessing the gate of their enemies were something the Church was to dispense as part of its administration, it would be distributed to the same individuals who receive other privileges, including hypocrites. However, Christ has not left such a legacy to the Church; His kingdom is not of this world. This promise declares what God will do as the sovereign ruler of all kingdoms, who "giveth it to whomsoever he will," (Daniel 4:17).

Furthermore, in the days when Abraham's seed will receive this power, the Church will have been brought to such a state of perfection that there will be few, if any, hypocrites within it. The power will effectively rest in the hands of the true seed of Abraham due to their predominance. The perfection of the Church during this time is described in many Scriptures. For example, Isaiah 60:21 says, "Thy people also shall be all righteous, they shall inherit the land forever, the branch of my planting, the work of my hands, that I may be glorified." Similarly, Isaiah 35:8 speaks of a way of holiness where, "the unclean shall not pass over it," and "the redeemed shall walk there." Revelation 21:27 states that, "there shall in no wise enter into it any thing that defileth," and Zechariah 14:21 declares that, "in that day there shall be no more the Canaanite in the house of the Lord of hosts."

In these promises, we see that in the time of the *Church's perfection*, the hypocrites and unclean will be excluded. Thus, when the seed of Abraham possesses the gates of their enemies, it will be a fulfillment of God's promise, accomplished in righteousness and with His chosen people.

From these passages, I do not assert that the Church will achieve absolute perfection or be entirely free from hypocrisy at that time, but I do affirm that it will attain a far greater degree of purity than it has yet reached. Moreover, whatever level of purity or perfection the Church may achieve, whether greater or lesser, the expressions in these prophecies clearly indicate that until the Church reaches a state of maturity and glory—worthy of the title "New Jerusalem descending from heaven, wherein righteousness dwells"—the people of God should not expect to possess that promised power. The reality is that, were such power entrusted to them in the Church's current condition, the many who would don the masks of hypocrisy and feigned sainthood to secure positions of influence would overshadow the true spiritual seed of Abraham. Such impostors, once in positions of power, would act in ways entirely unbecoming of saints, their refined outward religion serving only to conceal their inner corruption. Thus, the Lord, who has indeed ordained this power for His people in this world, has wisely reserved it until they are adequately prepared to receive and exercise it, as He declares in Isaiah 60:22, "I the Lord will hasten it in his time."

From this, it is evident that despite the objections raised, the promise of this power is intended for the true spiritual seed of Abraham, not for pretenders. When that day comes, the power will naturally and justly fall into their hands, causing no distress about its placement.

Before moving on, let me offer a caution to prevent misunderstanding. Until the time comes when the "New Jerusalem descends from heaven," it should not be presumed that the people of God must lay aside their swords or refrain from participating in the governance and defense of their nations. Nor should they abstain from being instruments in advancing God's kingdom through lawful means, including, at times, the use of force in so far as it aligns with God's purposes. However, when the fullness of power is bestowed upon them in accordance with prophecy, it will come to them justly and naturally, arising from principles of equity and reason, as previously discussed. Until that time, in serving their country, believers should act as loyal citizens, involved in the common interests of their nation or society. Their sainthood may qualify them for certain responsibilities and, in elections, may commend them for positions of trust. However, their sainthood does not entitle them to civil authority or power. As Christ Himself declared, "My kingdom is not of this world," and it never shall be, as has already been demonstrated.

If power and government were to be granted to saints solely, on the basis of their sainthood, we would require a much greater ability to discern who the saints truly are. To address this difficulty, those who have claimed such a privilege have often relied on supposed revelations from heaven to validate their authority. This practice, however, is manifestly absurd and disruptive in a civil society. Justice in a commonwealth must be publicly understood and recognized by the community or its majority. For this reason, a supposed revelation from heaven, even if true, cannot serve as evidence in a civil court. Unless the judge also receives a revelation, it lies outside the realm of his understanding. Even if both judge and witnesses claimed to have received the same revelation, the sentence could not rest upon it, as the judgment of a court must represent the will of the commonwealth, supported by its power to enforce the ruling. It is worth considering whether this principle may have been why Cain was not executed for murdering Abel, as the crime, committed secretly in the field, was revealed only by the Lord Himself. Matters subject to civil judgment must fall within the bounds of human sense or reason.

One additional point remains to be addressed, forming a *seventh* application of this teaching: the responsibility of God's people to actively seek the advancement of His kingdom.

As we have seen, the way to advance this kingdom is for believers to strive to increase the number of God's people. To this end, they must endeavor to be blessings within their families, to their nation, and to the communities where they live. They should work to nurture the hearts of their children, servants, friends, and neighbors with the knowledge and love of Christ. Although this work is vast and beyond human strength or the efficacy of instruction and example alone, believers must trust in God's ability to fulfill His promise. He has declared that He will make believers blessings to families and nations and that, through their multiplication, they will possess the gates of their enemies. With this in view, believers should commit themselves to being blessings in these ways.

First, be careful not to violate Abraham's covenant, as those do, who deny the application of its seal to infants, as has been demonstrated from Genesis 17. In doing so, they, as far as it lies within their power, *nullify and invalidate that promise*. To defend this error, such individuals often deny the *extent* of that promise.

Let it never be said or thought by me that none who hold this belief are blessings to families or nations. I firmly believe that many of them are holy, sincere, and dear to Christ, who overlooks the errors and weaknesses of His people and uses even such individuals, despite their mistake, as instruments of much good. Yet, based on the discussion of this point, I must assert that those who forbid little children from being brought to Christ are, in this matter, *not true friends to His kingdom*. In this regard, they take a path that hinders their ability to be blessings to families or nations. Neglecting the right way of advancing His kingdom and exalting His throne in the world, they adopt unnatural, unsafe, and false methods, which lead to predictable and undesirable outcomes. Instead of establishing His kingdom, they unknowingly advance something else, which brings no blessing.

It is the blessing of God upon individuals, not their abilities—however great—that enables them to be active blessings to others, particularly in managing the affairs of His kingdom, which is a blessed kingdom. God bestows blessings according to His covenant, as everything He has ever done or continues to do for His people is based on a covenant. While we may consider the omission of an ordinance or duty within the covenant to be a small matter,

God views it differently, often responding by granting or withholding His blessing and leaving marks of His displeasure upon those who transgress in such things.

As you seek to be blessings to families and nations, claiming the privilege afforded by Abraham's covenant, you must *also follow in Abraham's steps*. The Apostle instructs, "Be not slothful, but followers of them who through faith and patience inherit the promises," (Hebrews 6:12). Jesus said, "If ye were Abraham's children, ye would do the works of Abraham," (John 8:39). This implies that inheriting Abraham's promise and blessing requires more than being his natural descendants. Do not expect to be blessings to your neighbors, children, or servants as Abraham was unless you follow his example in three specific ways.

First, you must teach your families as Abraham did. God said, "I know him, that he will command his children and his household after him, and they shall keep the way of the Lord, to do justice and judgment; that the Lord may bring upon Abraham that which he hath spoken of him," (Genesis 18:19). This implies that if family duties are neglected, the promise will not be fulfilled. God accomplishes sanctification by involving His people in the process and making them active participants. He bestows such blessings through means, choosing those most appropriate and effective for achieving His purposes. Among all means of grace, family instruction and example are especially effective, preparing individuals to benefit from public preaching, particularly the young. The authority, example, and influence of parents or household leaders provide a significant advantage, fostering attentiveness, readiness to hear, and a deeper consideration of Gospel truths. Mutual respect and love within families enhance these efforts, making them fruitful. God, recognizing the potential of His saints to bring others to Him—especially those under their care—has promised to bless such endeavors. This is why Joshua could declare, "Choose ye this day whom ye will serve... but as for me and my house, we will serve the Lord," (Joshua 24:15). Timothy, too, knew the Scriptures from childhood because, "the same faith dwelt in his grandmother Lois and his mother Eunice," (2 Timothy 1:5, 2 Timothy 3:15). Similarly, Solomon was instructed by his mother. Following Abraham's example in teaching your family is essential to advancing Christ's kingdom.

Second, you must emulate Abraham's uprightness and sincerity in serving God. God commanded, "Walk before me, and be thou upright, and I will make my covenant between me and thee, and will multiply thee exceedingly," (Genesis 17:1). Scripture also declares, "The generation of the upright shall be blessed," (Psalm 112:2). Much of a Christian's work in walking with God involves family duties. If these duties are performed merely out of formality, with a desire to appear religious, little good will come of them. While a form of godliness is better than none, it lacks the power to make a lasting impact. However, one who genuinely seeks to glorify God and save the souls of those around him is truly a blessing. Sincere and heartfelt efforts carry greater authority and influence, as they resonate with others' hearts and leave a deeper impression. A Christian who is merely formal is like salt that has lost its savor—it cannot season.

Third, you must strive to be a friend of God, as Abraham was. This requires being *spiritual and heavenly-minded*, walking closely with God, and observing His dealings with you. You must seek to please Him in all things, gain His love, and grow in favor with Him. Those who maintain a close relationship with God are blessings wherever they go. Jesus likened such individuals to leaven, capable of influencing those around them with the fear and love of Christ. A person who frequently communes with God develops a humble, meek, and gracious spirit, rich in faith, and exuding the presence of God in their conduct. Their example curbs wickedness and encourages holiness. As a friend of the Bridegroom, they are instrumental in bringing souls into Christ's arms. Conversely, those who neglect this relationship with God are ill-equipped to be spiritual blessings, especially to those closest to them, who observe their ways most closely. A friend of both the Bridegroom and the Bride must *first be a friend of God*.

FINIS.

Sufficiency and Superiority
By C. Matthew McMahon, Ph.D., Th.D.

Psalm 33:9, "For he spake, and it was done; He commanded, and it stood fast."

When a man gets to speaking about what he can do, the whole world usually has to sit down, wait a spell, and see if he makes good on it—or if he's just talk. But here, we're not dealing with a man. No committee meeting, no delays, no need for elbow grease. It's simple: God speaks, and creation snaps to attention like a soldier to his captain. Light floods in, seas get their marching orders, and mountains set themselves down like they've been told to stay put. There's no haggling or second-guessing. It's done because He said so, and that's all there is to it.

Now, I've seen people in my day try to bend the world to their will—grand speeches, big plans, sweat on their brows—but it all hangs on shaky scaffolding. The real marvel is that the Maker of all things doesn't have to lift a finger. One command, and it all stands firm, like it's been there forever. That's power the likes of which you can't find in the whole of the Tennessee mountains—or anywhere else. And it's a good thing, too, because if that same Word can steady the cosmos, it's sure enough a foundation worth leaning on for all of us who are wobbling through life in this fallen world. This has a direct correlation to William Carter's work.

In examining the *way* God reveals Himself to His people, William Carter's work, *The Manifestation of God to His*

People in the Last Days, rests on the undeniable truth that God has spoken *fully* and *finally* in His Son, Jesus Christ. From this central truth, two key points emerge: the superiority of revelation through Christ and the sufficiency of Scripture. These truths, solidly grounded in Hebrews 1:1-2, provide a rich foundation for understanding the Word of God and its rightful place in the life of believers.

"God, who at sundry times and in divers manners spake in time past unto the fathers by the prophets, hath in these last days spoken unto us by his Son," (Hebrews 1:1-2). In these opening verses of Hebrews, Carter uncovers a stark contrast between how God revealed Himself before and after the coming of Christ. The Old Testament saints received God's Word "piece after piece," through dreams, visions, and other extraordinary means. But in the fullness of time, God sent His own Son, who is the exact image of the Father, to reveal His will perfectly and completely.

The old ways of revelation, while genuine and necessary for their time, were limited in scope and partial in content. The prophets, though inspired by the Holy Spirit, spoke in fragments—a promise here, a vision there—always pointing forward to something greater. For instance, the promise to Adam and Eve that the seed of the woman would crush the serpent's head was a shadowy glimpse of redemption. Abraham saw the day of Christ afar off, but it was only a distant vision. Moses spoke of a prophet like himself who would arise, but he could not fully unfold the details of His mission. These glimpses were valuable, yet they left much unrevealed.

When Christ came, the shadows fled before the light. Typology was completed and finished. He is the "brightness of his glory, and the express image of his person," (Hebrews 1:3), revealing the fullness of God's will and character. In Christ, God has spoken everything necessary for salvation, life, and godliness. The revelation given in His Son is not piecemeal but *complete*. As the Apostle Paul declares, "Having made known unto us the mystery of his will, according to his good pleasure which he hath purposed in himself," (Ephesians 1:9). What was hidden for ages has now been unveiled.

This superior revelation means that the old ways of receiving God's Word are *no longer needed*. The dreams, visions, and extraordinary measures used in times past served their purpose, but now the Son has come. To seek after such methods today is to misunderstand the sufficiency and finality of Christ's revelation. As Carter puts it, the rising of the Sun of Righteousness has rendered the stars of the old ways *unnecessary*. The saints of the New Testament era are no longer children under guardians and tutors but are now heirs of the full inheritance. The darkness is past, and the true light now shines (1 John 2:8).

Flowing naturally from the superiority of Christ's revelation is the sufficiency of Scripture. Carter affirms that the Bible contains everything needed to know God and live for Him. The Word of God, written by holy men under the "carrying along" of the Holy Spirit, preserves and declares the full revelation given through Christ (that which is inspired). "All scripture is given by inspiration of God, and is profitable for doctrine, for reproof, for correction, for instruction in righteousness," (2 Timothy 3:16).

This sufficiency means that Christians must not seek after *new* revelations or visions. The canon of Scripture is closed, and all that God intends for His people to know has been recorded in its pages. To look for additional words from God undermines the completeness of what He has already given. Carter warns that such pursuits lead to spiritual instability and open the door to deception. The Spirit's work is not to add to the Word but to illuminate and apply it to the hearts of believers.

The sufficiency of Scripture does not mean it is an easy book to master. On the contrary, it demands study, meditation, and prayerful dependence on the Holy Spirit. Carter compares the Scriptures to a mine rich with treasures, requiring diligent effort to extract its wealth. "Search the scriptures," Christ commanded, "for in them ye think ye have eternal life, and they are they which testify of me," (John 5:39). The work of searching is not optional for believers; it is the very means by which they grow in grace and in the knowledge of Christ.

Carter also emphasizes the communal nature of Scripture study. Ministers, though fallible, are appointed by God to teach His Word. Their task is not to proclaim new truths but to faithfully explain and apply what is already revealed. Christians are called to test all teaching against Scripture, ensuring that it aligns with the truth. The Bereans provide an example of this noble practice, "These were more noble than those in Thessalonica, in that they received the word with all readiness of mind, and searched the scriptures daily, whether those things were so," (Acts 17:11).

The sufficiency of Scripture also demands that believers reject any reliance on mere outward forms. Carter warns against treating the Word as a dead letter or engaging in empty rituals. Instead, Christians must receive the Word with faith and obedience, allowing it to transform their hearts and lives. The Spirit accompanies the Word, sanctifying believers and conforming them to the image of Christ. Through the Scriptures, God works to mortify sin, strengthen faith, and provide comfort and assurance.

Carter's insights into the superiority of revelation through Christ and the sufficiency of Scripture align beautifully with Reformed orthodoxy (and the *1647 Westminster Standards*). They affirm the centrality of Christ in God's redemptive plan and the complete reliability of the Scriptures as the rule of faith and life. These truths guard against the errors of mysticism, which seeks truth apart from Scripture, and the dangers of legalism, which reduces faith to external observances.

The Reformed tradition rightly holds Scripture as the ultimate authority because it is God's Word (see the *1647 Westminster Confession of Faith* chapter 1!). The sufficiency of Scripture ensures that every believer, through the Spirit's work, has all of the full riches of divine truth given to them. This process and blessing of spiritual knowledge does not abolish the role of ministers but situates them as servants of the Word rather than lords over the faith of others. It also encourages a vibrant, living faith rooted in the Word, where believers engage with Scripture not merely to know about God but to know Him personally.

Carter's emphasis on Christ as the supreme revelation calls believers to fix their eyes on Him as the Author and Finisher of their faith (Hebrews 12:2). The shadows of the Old Testament have given way to the substance found in Christ. To seek after other means of revelation is to *miss* the glory of what has *already* been given. In Christ, believers have all they need for life and godliness (2 Peter 1:3).

In exploring the divine revelation given through Christ and its application to believers, Carter outlines two further pillars of truth: the Spirit's work of sanctification in believers and the ordained role of ministers in proclaiming God's Word. These truths build upon the sufficiency of Scripture and the completeness of Christ's revelation, providing a clear picture of how God works through His Word and His people.

Sanctification, as Carter describes, is a hallmark of the Spirit's work in the believer. It is through the Word of God that the Spirit carries out this work, setting apart the believer for holy purposes. Christ's own words affirm this: "Sanctify them through thy truth: thy word is truth," (John 17:17). The Word, therefore, is not merely a static text but a living and active instrument through which the Spirit transforms the hearts and lives of God's people.

The Spirit accomplishes this sanctifying work in three primary ways. First, it brings the soul under the power of God's truth. This is no small task, for the natural man resists divine authority. Sanctification involves a willing surrender of every faculty to God, a submission that can only come by the Spirit's enabling. Just as a gardener prunes a vine to make it fruitful, the Spirit cuts away self-will and sin to align the believer's mind and heart with the truth.

Second, *enter sanctification*. Sanctification breaks the power of sin's corruption. As Carter reminds us, sin clouds the understanding and hardens the heart, leading men to reject God's Word. But the Spirit, working through the Word, cleanses the soul and enables it to embrace the truth. The Apostle Paul puts it plainly: "Be ye transformed by the renewing of your mind, that ye may prove what is that good, and acceptable, and perfect, will of God," (Romans 12:2). Sanctification involves this renewal, freeing the believer from the entanglements of sin and enabling a clearer view of God's will.

Third, sanctification impresses upon the soul the power of God's truth. As the Spirit applies the Word, the believer experiences its life-giving force. This is not a mere intellectual exercise but a profound encounter with the living God. The Word not only informs but transforms, shaping the believer into the image of Christ. This transformative power testifies to the divine origin of Scripture, for no human wisdom could accomplish such a work.

Sanctification through the Word also bears witness to the sufficiency of Scripture. It is through diligent study, meditation, and prayer that believers grow in holiness. Carter likens this to mining for treasure—a laborious but rewarding endeavor. To neglect the Word is to forfeit the Spirit's sanctifying work, leaving the soul vulnerable to sin and error. Thus, believers are called to, "work out [*their*] own salvation with fear and trembling," (Philippians 2:12), trusting that it is God who works in them to will and to do for His good pleasure. He uses ministers to preach his word in this way. The central task of a minister is the faithful proclamation of God's Word. This involves not only preaching but also teaching, exhorting, and discipling. Ministers are to "rightly divide the word of truth," (2 Timothy 2:15), ensuring that their teaching aligns with Scripture. They are also to model godliness, serving as examples to the flock (1 Peter 5:3).

In the final sections of the work, two critical themes emerge: the necessity of ordinary means for spiritual growth and the role of human effort in acquiring the knowledge of God. These points highlight God's design in using common, accessible tools for extraordinary purposes and call believers to active engagement with the means He has provided.

These means include the preaching and teaching of Scripture, prayer, the sacraments, and fellowship among believers. Each of these tools is grounded in God's Word and serves as a channel (*the means of grace*) through which the Spirit works. Carter likens them to a well from which believers draw the living water of God's truth. To neglect these means is to turn away from the provision God has made, leaving the soul parched and unfruitful.

The cessation of extraordinary revelations does not signal a lack of divine activity but rather a *maturing* of the Church. Carter explains that, in the time of the Old Testament, the Church was in its infancy and required additional guidance through dreams, visions, and direct prophetic utterances. Now, in the fullness of time, God's Word has been revealed in Christ, providing everything necessary for life and godliness (2 Peter 1:3). The ordinary means are sufficient because they are empowered by the Spirit, who applies the truth of God's Word to the hearts of believers.

While salvation is entirely a work of God's grace, Carter emphasizes that believers are called to active participation in their spiritual growth (which is discernable). This effort is not an attempt to earn favor with God but a response to His grace. As Paul exhorts, "Work out your own salvation with fear and trembling. For it is God which worketh in you both to will and to do of his good pleasure," (Philippians 2:12-13).

Carter identifies three primary ways in which human effort is essential in the pursuit of knowing God. First, believers must diligently *search* the Scriptures. The Bible is described as a treasure chest of divine wisdom, and discovering its riches requires intentional effort. Carter admonishes believers not to approach the Word passively but to engage with it as one digging for hidden gold. "If thou seekest her as silver, and searchest for her as for hid treasures; then shalt thou understand the fear of the Lord, and find the knowledge of God," (Proverbs 2:4-5).

Second, believers must *persevere* in prayer. Prayer is not only a means of communing with God but also a way to seek His guidance and illumination. Carter views prayer as the lifeblood of the Christian life, sustaining the soul and enabling believers to apply the truths of Scripture. Christ

Himself modeled this dependence on prayer, often withdrawing to solitary places to seek His Father's will (Mark 1:35). In the same way, believers are called to, "pray without ceasing," (1 Thessalonians 5:17), trusting that God will answer and provide according to His perfect wisdom.

Third, believers must actively participate in the life of the Church. The community of faith is an essential means through which God works. Carter describes the Church as a body, with each member contributing to the growth and health of the whole. Fellowship with other believers provides accountability, encouragement, and opportunities to practice love and service. The Apostle Paul writes, "Let us consider one another to provoke unto love and to good works, not forsaking the assembling of ourselves together, as the manner of some is; but exhorting one another," (Hebrews 10:24-25).

Carter's teaching strikes a careful balance between God's sovereignty and human responsibility. While the Spirit's work is indispensable, believers are not passive recipients but active participants in their sanctification. This cooperation reflects the nature of God's relationship with His people, one that invites their full engagement while ultimately resting on His power and faithfulness.

While the means themselves are ordinary, their effectiveness lies in the Spirit's power. Carter points to John 16:13: "When he, the Spirit of truth, is come, he will guide you into all truth: for he shall not speak of himself; but whatsoever he shall hear, that shall he speak: and he will shew you things to come." The Spirit's role is not to provide new revelations but to illuminate the truth already revealed in Christ. Through the preaching of the Word, the Spirit convicts, comforts, and transforms hearts.

The ordinary means of grace—Scripture, prayer, and fellowship—are not mere rituals but vital channels through which God reveals Himself and conforms His people to the image of Christ. In embracing these means, believers can rest assured that they are participating in God's grand design, growing in faith, and glorifying Him in all things.

Added to Carter's "Short Discourse" on this subject, is also two sermons that follow, "Light in Darkness" and "Israel's Peace with God."

In *Light in Darkness*, Carter delivers a stirring sermon that calls both the leaders of his day and the faithful at large to reflect deeply on the workings of God's hand in their lives and labors. Preached before the House of Commons during a time of national uncertainty, this message lays bare the truth that God often answers the prayers of His people "by terrible things in righteousness" (Psalm 65:5). Carter insists that the trials and hardships encountered in God's service are not haphazard but purposeful, refining the believer and ensuring the advancement of His glory and kingdom.

He challenges his audience to approach their work for God with spiritual hearts, untainted by selfish ambition or pride. He reminds them that the success of their endeavors lies not in the avoidance of difficulty but in steadfastly acting according to God's will, trusting Him even amid opposition and affliction. Drawing from vivid scriptural examples, he illustrates how God's people, from Moses in the wilderness to the Canaanite woman pleading before Christ, found their comfort and salvation not in avoiding trials but in trusting God through them.

The sermon concludes with a call to unity, humility, and self-examination, warning against strife and bitterness among believers. It invites all to, "work out your salvation with fear and trembling," (Philippians 2:12), urging faithfulness in every endeavor for God. Carter's words endure as a reminder that even in darkness, the hand of God is at work, shaping His people for eternal good.

The sermon on the Benjamites called *Israel's Peace with God*, presents a solemn and urgent appeal to consider how God's work prospers only in the hands of those whose sins are forgiven and whose peace with Him is secure. Drawing on the biblical account in Judges 20:26-28, where Israel is repeatedly defeated in battle until they humble themselves, seek pardon, and offer sacrifices, the preacher emphasizes that divine blessing follows true repentance and reconciliation.

This message explores the nature of sin, describing its power as rooted in human nature, producing destruction in its fruit, and requiring nothing less than Christ's atoning blood for its cure. The preacher brings this reality to bear with sharp clarity, urging his audience to lament their offenses against God, weep over their transgressions, and turn to Christ for mercy. The congregation is exhorted to commit fully to the covenant of God, presenting themselves as living sacrifices and refusing to falter in their duty.

This sermon serves as a vital reminder of the practical outworking of the Christian faith, showing that faith without action is lifeless and that spiritual negligence dishonors God and imperils souls. Anchored in the hope of forgiveness and the strength of God's promises, it calls the hearers to labor in God's service, confident that, "the ways of the Lord are right, and the just shall walk in them," (Hosea 14:9). The work of the Lord, grounded in righteousness and grace, is certain to prevail through the faithful obedience of His people.

In Christ's grace and mercy,
C. Matthew McMahon, Ph.D., Th.D.
From My study, February, 2025
"...search the Scriptures..." (John 5:39).
www.apuritansmind.com
www.puritanpublications.com
www.gracechapeltn.com
www.reformedsynod.com

A Short Discourse

A Short Discourse Concerning the Manifestations of God to His People in the Last Days

Herein it is shown how the Spirit works in ordinary gifts rather than through extraordinary revelations.

Hebrews 1:1: *"God, who at sundry times and in divers manners spoke in times past unto the fathers by the prophets, hath in these last days spoken unto us by his Son."*

These words present a comparison between the manifestations of God to His people before and after the coming of Christ. This, in general, is the Apostle's purpose: for when he says, "In these last days, God hath spoken unto us by His Son," the word "us" does not merely refer to those who heard Christ speaking in person. This could not be entirely true of all those to whom the Apostle wrote this epistle, as not everyone had heard Christ directly. If that had been his intent, he would have written, "To some of us He hath spoken by His Son."

Furthermore, the Apostle speaks of these times and people in the same way elsewhere, as in 1 Corinthians 10:11, "Upon us the ends of the world are come." We find similar language in 1 Timothy 4:1, 2 Timothy 3:1, 1 Peter 1:20, and Hebrews 9:26. Therefore, by "us in these last days," he refers to the people of God under the New Testament, from Christ's time until the end of the world.

This is further supported by the distinction he makes between "us" and "the fathers." By "the fathers," he refers to the people of the many ages before Christ. By "us in these last days," he means the people of the many ages after Christ's coming in the flesh. Thus, the scope of these words is to show the differing light granted in the former and latter ages of the world.

Particulars of the Comparison

1. What is similar between the two eras: the Author of the Manifestation: The same God has spoken to both them and us. It is the same God of the Old and New Testaments, speaking things that only He could declare. Therefore, in studying the Scriptures, neither the Old nor the New Testament should be neglected.

The Nature of the Manifestation: God spoke to both them and us, not directly but through intermediaries. In the past, He spoke through prophets, and in these last days, He has spoken through His Son, who is both God and man. Although God could have communicated without any messenger or external means, His chosen way has always been to convey His treasures through human vessels. As Isaiah 57:19 says, "I create the fruit of the lips; peace, peace to him that is far off, and to him that is near."

2. What differs between the two eras: Regarding the fathers: God spoke to them through prophets, men inspired by the Holy Spirit. As stated in 2 Peter 1:21, "Holy men of

God spoke as they were moved by the Holy Ghost." God's messages to them were delivered progressively—piecemeal—at different times. For instance, something was revealed to Adam and Eve in the promise that, "the seed of the woman shall bruise the serpent's head." Later, more was revealed to Abraham, then to Moses, and subsequently to other prophets. These messages were conveyed in diverse ways: through dreams, visions, the Urim and Thummim, and other extraordinary methods.

Regarding us in these last days: God has spoken to us directly through His Son, not through other intermediaries. While God spoke to the fathers piece by piece, through many prophets and over time, He has spoken to us all at once through His Son. In Christ, He has revealed the full mystery of His will, which was hidden from ages and generations but is now made manifest to the saints (Colossians 1:26). Unlike the extraordinary means used in the past—dreams, visions, and the like—God now speaks to us exclusively through His Son.

These distinctions imply that Christ's role as God's messenger replaces the former extraordinary means of revelation. The opposition is not between extraordinary means of the past and ordinary means now, for God still manifests Himself in ordinary ways today, piece by piece. The difference lies in the extraordinary nature of the revelations: then through prophets and diverse methods, now solely through Christ. By "extraordinary," we refer to what is beyond the ordinary experiences of believers.

The principle is this: while in the times before Christ, God spoke to the fathers through prophets who were extraordinarily inspired by the Holy Spirit and through diverse revelations, in these last days such extraordinary means and prophets have ceased. God has spoken to us solely through His Son. Any further understanding of God's will must now be attained through ordinary gifts, by searching and studying what the Son has revealed.

To better understand the Apostle's meaning when he says God, "spoke by the prophets" and "has spoken by His Son," we must first *clarify* this expression. It does not merely refer to literal speech or audible words. The prophets sometimes conveyed God's message through signs, and Christ did so not only by words but also by actions. For example, it is said in Hebrews 12:24, "His blood speaketh." During His earthly ministry, Christ spoke audibly to only a few, yet His speaking in the text extends to us, as shown earlier, upon whom, "the ends of the world are come," (1 Corinthians 10:11).

When the Apostle refers to God speaking by the prophets, he means *the entire revelation* of God conveyed to His saints through them, whether by word or other means, as recorded in the Old Testament. Similarly, when he says God has spoken by His Son, he refers to the full manifestation of God through Jesus Christ—not only in His words but also in His incarnation, death, resurrection, ascension, and His entire work as Mediator. These acts are recorded and explained in the New Testament.

This is why the Apostle Paul says the purpose of his ministry was, "to give the light of the knowledge of the glory of God in the face of Christ," (2 Corinthians 4:6). The Apostles' ministry was part of Christ's speaking, as they revealed God's truth only as seen in Christ. This does not refer to Christ's natural, physical face, for He had already ascended, but to the entire narrative of His life and work as set forth in the writings of the New Testament. Paul also emphasizes this when he says the focus of his preaching was, "Christ crucified," (1 Corinthians 1:23), and the essence of Gospel teaching is learning Christ (Ephesians 4:20). In this way, Christ's speaking involves both words and deeds as they are recorded in the New Testament.

The Role of Extraordinary Revelations

If someone objects that extraordinary revelations occurred even during the time of Christ's speaking, as seen in the Apostles' ministry, the answer is clear: what the Apostles and other early witnesses did was part of Christ's speaking. Their work was, the means by which Christ conveyed the manifestation of God. When the Apostle contrasts Christ's speaking with the extraordinary methods used by prophets in former times, he does not deny that Christ's speaking was extraordinary. Rather, he emphasizes that Christ's speaking was completed and confirmed by witnesses chosen by God and attested by miracles and gifts of the Holy Spirit (Hebrews 2:3-4). After this confirmation, such extraordinary methods ceased to be used.

Objection: Why Wasn't Speaking by Prophets Before Christ Considered Speaking by the Son? It might be argued that if speaking by messengers during Christ's time is considered speaking by the Son, then speaking by prophets before His coming should also be considered speaking by the Son, especially since the Old Testament prophets were messengers of Christ. For instance, Hebrews 8:8 states that Christ gave the New Covenant, and Hebrews 9:16 confirms it was sealed with His blood. Additionally, 1 Peter 1:11 says the Spirit of Christ was in the prophets, revealing what was to come.

To this, I respond: 1. It is true that the Spirit of Christ spoke in the prophets and that they were sent by Christ, the Son of God. However, Christ was not revealed then as He is now. Paul himself says he was chosen by God, "to reveal His Son in me," (Galatians 1:16). The Gospel of John describes those earlier times as when, "the light shined in darkness, and the darkness comprehended it not," (John 1:5). Additionally, the message was not delivered in the Son's name as it is now. As Paul says, "We are ambassadors for Christ," (2 Corinthians 5:20). Therefore, though the Spirit of Christ spoke through the prophets, this was not the same as the speaking by the Son mentioned here.

2. In the Old Testament, God spoke through messengers alone. Now, Christ Himself has *come* and *spoken*. The manifestation of God through Christ is not only conveyed by His words but also through His very being and actions. The work of the prophets was to declare what the Spirit of Christ revealed to them. In contrast, the Apostles

and New Testament writers were tasked with unveiling and explaining what Christ, through His life and work of redemption, had said and done. This is why Paul refers to it as the revelation of the Son in him and the preaching of Christ crucified. For this reason, though some of Christ's speaking has been conveyed by messengers, it is still considered speaking by the Son in a unique way that Old Testament prophecy was not.

The New Testament as the Full Manifestation

This speaking by the Son encompasses all the Scriptures of the New Testament, including the Gospels (which recount His words and deeds), the Epistles (which explain them), and Revelation (which prophesies). It also encompasses the Old Testament, as Christ came to fulfill the Law and the Prophets. What was spoken in the Old Testament in a veiled manner has been spoken again with clarity in the New Testament, as it is often said: "The New Testament is veiled in the Old, and the Old is revealed in the New."

The essence of this teaching is that the entirety of God's revelation is contained in Scripture. We should not expect further extraordinary revelations. Any deeper understanding of God's truth must come through the use of ordinary gifts, by studying and searching out the mind of God as revealed through His Son.

The Final Period of God's Revelation

The phrase, "in these last days" in Hebrews 1:1 implies distinct periods in history: from Adam to Moses, from Moses to Christ, and from Christ to the end of the world. These periods are marked by the degrees of God's self-revelation. Since ours is the final period, we should not expect new extraordinary manifestations of God but rely on what has been given through His Son, as stated: "In these last days, He hath spoken unto us by His Son." This aligns with the parable in Matthew 21:37, where the master, after sending messengers, finally sends his son and no one else.

As Christ Himself said, "All that I have heard of my Father, I have declared unto you," (John 15:15), and "No man hath seen God at any time; the only begotten Son, who is in the bosom of the Father, He hath declared Him," (John 1:18). This underscores that Christ's work, as recorded in Scripture, is the complete and final revelation of God to mankind.

A further evidence of this truth is found in the text itself, in the second note of difference mentioned earlier: that while God spoke to the prophets of old in fragments—piecemeal and at various times—He has now spoken to us through one Prophet, His Son, revealing everything He had to say all at once. Through Christ, the entire mystery of His will has been disclosed, as it says in Ephesians 1:9, "Having made known unto us the mystery of his will, according to his good pleasure which he hath purposed in himself," and in Colossians 1:26, "Even the mystery which hath been hid from ages and from generations, but now is made manifest to his saints."

Thus, no more can be done to uncover the secrets of God's love, or the heights and depths of His mercy, goodness, and wisdom, beyond what the Son has already revealed. As Solomon once said, "What can the man do that cometh after the king? Even that which hath been already done." In the same way, nothing greater or additional can be expected beyond what has been revealed through the Son's speaking.

This is also the meaning of Jude 1:3, where the Apostle exhorts believers to, "contend for the faith which was once delivered unto the saints." The phrase "once delivered," indicates that it was delivered in full, so nothing more should be added. Thus, when faith is lost or endangered, as some have made shipwreck of it, the instruction is not to seek new revelations to restore or confirm it but to contend for what has already been received. The same sense of "once" appears in Hebrews 9:28, "So Christ was once offered to bear the sins of many," and in Hebrews 10:10, "We are sanctified through the offering of the body of Jesus Christ once for all." Likewise, in Hebrews 7:27, it says Christ does not need to offer sacrifices daily, as the high priests did, because, "this he did once, when he offered up himself." These passages teach that Christ's single offering was *complete and perfect*, accomplishing what all the previous sacrifices could not. Similarly, His one revelation surpasses everything communicated by the prophets in the past. Since God's manifestation has now been given in full through His Son, no other way of revelation is to be expected.

This is further supported by John 16:13-14, where Jesus says, "When the Spirit of truth is come, he will guide you into all truth, for he shall not speak of himself; but whatsoever he shall hear, that shall he speak: and he will show you things to come. He shall glorify me, for he shall receive of mine and shall show it unto you." These words describe the work of the Spirit and the way He would operate in believers after Christ's ascension. Jesus spoke these words to His disciples, addressing them not only as Apostles but as believers, to comfort them concerning His departure. He said, "Because I have said these things unto you, sorrow hath filled your heart. Nevertheless, I tell you the truth; it is expedient for you that I go away: for if I go not away, the Comforter will not come unto you," (John 16:6-7). He then described the work of the Comforter, saying, "When he is come, he will reprove the world of sin, and of righteousness, and of judgment," (John 16:8). These functions apply universally to believers and are not limited to the Apostles, as nothing in this passage speaks specifically of their apostolic office.

Therefore, this description of the Spirit's work applies to believers until the end of the world. If any extraordinary revelations were still to be expected, they would have to come through the Spirit. Yet Jesus clarifies that the Spirit's role is not to introduce new doctrine but to guide believers into truth already revealed through the Son. When Jesus says, "He shall guide you into all truth," the Greek word for "guide" implies that the believer must also act, exerting effort to follow the Spirit's leading.

Furthermore, Jesus adds, "He shall not speak of himself; but whatsoever he shall hear, that shall he speak: and he will show you things to come." This means the Spirit will not deliver a new doctrine independently of Christ. Instead, the Spirit's work is to build upon Christ's foundation, helping believers understand what Christ has already spoken and revealed.

Jesus emphasizes this point, saying, "He shall glorify me, for he shall receive of mine, and shall show it unto you." The Spirit brings honor to Christ by taking what Christ has revealed and demonstrating it to believers, but nothing beyond that. The Spirit does not depart from the teachings of Christ or the Scriptures to introduce anything new. As Paul writes, "For God, who commanded the light to shine out of darkness, hath shined in our hearts, to give the light of the knowledge of the glory of God in the face of Jesus Christ," (2 Corinthians 4:6). The Son's work was to reveal; the Spirit's work is to demonstrate what has been revealed. As Paul also says, "My speech and my preaching was not with enticing words of man's wisdom, but in demonstration of the Spirit and of power," (1 Corinthians 2:4). It is through the hearing of faith that believers receive the Spirit (Galatians 3:2), and this work is not accomplished through visions or extraordinary revelations as in the days of the prophets, but through the ordinary means of understanding and applying what Christ has already spoken.

Objection 1. But you may say, as it is stated in John 16:12, "I have yet many things to say unto you, but ye cannot bear them now. Howbeit when he, the Spirit of truth, is come, he will guide you into all truth." This seems to imply that there were things the Spirit would reveal that Christ had not yet disclosed.

Answer. First, the meaning is not that Christ had left the mystery of His Father's will incomplete, for He explicitly states in John 15:15, "All things that I have heard of my Father I have made known unto you." Rather, it refers to a fuller and more detailed understanding of what He had already revealed, which the Spirit would provide after His ascension. Christ declared that the Spirit would not speak independently but would take what belonged to Him and show it to us.

Secondly, the speaking of the Son, as mentioned in the text, encompasses more than what is intended in John 16:12. In John 16:12, Christ refers specifically to what He had spoken in words to His disciples. However, in the text, the speaking of the Son includes the entire manifestation of God through Christ, both in words and actions. Thus, while it may be true that Christ did not speak certain things directly in words, the whole revelation of God in His life, works, and teachings contains everything the Spirit would later illuminate.

Objection 2. It is said in John 16:13, "The Spirit shall guide you into all truth, and show you things to come," which appears to limit this promise to the Apostles, as it is not true of all believers that they are led into all truth or shown things to come.

Answer. This same principle applies to all believers, as we see in 1 John 2:20, where the Apostle writes to

Christians of all ages and says, "Ye have an unction from the Holy One, and ye know all things." This does not mean that every believer, even the "little children" mentioned in verse 13, possesses perfect knowledge, for if that were true, there would have been no need for the Apostle to write to warn them about those who would seduce them (v. 26). Even the Apostles themselves were not led into all truth in the sense of knowing everything, for Paul says, "We know in part," (1 Corinthians 13:9).

The meaning, then, is that it is the Spirit's role and work to lead believers into truth, piece by piece, and into all truth ultimately. The Church as a whole will be led into all truth over time by the Spirit. As far as believers are led by the Spirit, they are led into truth, though this remains partial in this life.

Regarding the Spirit showing things to come, this also applies to all believers, as they are enabled by the Spirit, through study of the Scriptures, to understand prophecies. These were previously sealed, even to the saints, but now, by the Spirit's work, the meaning of these prophecies is revealed. Revelation 5 and 6 depict the Lamb opening the sealed book of prophecies. By fulfilling the prophecies concerning Himself, Christ enables believers in these last days to understand them as they pertain to His Church, the mystical body. Revelation 5:9 says, "Thou art worthy to take the book, and to open the seals thereof, for thou wast slain, and hast redeemed us to God by thy blood, and hast made us unto our God kings and priests." This is the declaration of the whole Church, represented by the four living creatures and the twenty-four elders, symbolizing all believers.

Another testimony to this doctrine is found in Hebrews 2:3-4: "How shall we escape, if we neglect so great salvation; which at the first began to be spoken by the Lord, and was confirmed unto us by them that heard him; God also bearing them witness, both with signs and wonders, and with divers miracles, and gifts of the Holy Ghost, according to his own will?" Here it is evident that the manifestation of salvation is from the Son, the Lord Christ.

The Apostles' role was to serve as witnesses and confirmers of this revelation, and they were equipped with miraculous gifts for that purpose. Once their testimony was confirmed, their office was no longer needed except through their writings. We cannot suppose that what the Son has spoken requires additional witnesses or further confirmation. For this reason, Christ is called "the Apostle and High Priest of our profession," (Hebrews 3:1), as all our guidance in religion comes from what He has spoken to us.

Thus, having established this truth, we must now consider why, though God possesses the same abundance of Spirit and could still speak to us through dreams, visions, extraordinary revelations, and infallibly inspired individuals, He has chosen not to do so. His people are just as precious to Him now as they were then, yet He has restricted us to what He has spoken through His Son, requiring us to seek the mind of God and the mystery of His will through the use and improvement of ordinary gifts.

Among the reasons that may be given for this, I will mention three.

Reason 1. Because His speaking to us by His Son has brought *greater* light into the world, rendering the former ways of revelation unnecessary and obsolete; just as when the sun rises, the stars disappear from sight. Christ is the "Sun of Righteousness," and since His rising, the saints have been placed in a better state, no longer needing the *types* of light that were necessary in earlier times. As it says in 1 John 2:8, "The darkness is past, and the true light now shineth."

During the infancy of the Church under the law, the saints required those earlier dispensations, and they were given to them. But since God has spoken to us by His Son, the Church has grown beyond its childlike state and no longer needs such means. The reason is that through the Son's revelation, the saints are now better equipped to discern the mind of God through diligent effort and the use of ordinary gifts, by studying and searching the Scriptures. The entire mystery of His will has now been revealed. Where the full truth of a matter is disclosed, each part sheds light on the others. This was not the case before Christ, as they had truth, but not its full revelation.

This is the meaning of John 1:18, "The law was given by Moses, but grace and truth came by Jesus Christ." This does not imply that the law was not true, as Psalm 119:142 declares, "Thy law is the truth." However, it was truth presented in types and shadows, much of it veiled and hidden, now revealed by Jesus Christ. The mystery kept hidden from ages and generations has been made manifest through Him. The law outlines the way, but the power is unveiled in the Gospel. The law speaks of life in God through His service, but it leaves unanswered questions, such as, "Who shall ascend into heaven?" or "Who shall descend into the deep?" The Gospel provides the answers, as explained in Romans 10:5-8.

Without the whole picture, a person cannot see deeply into a matter or make a complete judgment. This was the state before Christ, which made prophets and extraordinary revelations necessary. But now, as the Apostle says, "We all, with open face, beholding as in a glass the glory of the Lord," (2 Corinthians 3:18).

When Jesus said in Matthew 11:11 that John the Baptist was greater than all the prophets before him, yet the least in the kingdom of God is greater than he, this does not refer to John's personal gifts or graces, as he excelled many in the kingdom. It refers instead to the state of knowledge regarding God and His will. The prophets themselves did not fully understand what they prophesied, but now those truths are understood more clearly, as noted in 1 Peter 1:11.

The ultimate purpose of God's speaking through His Son was to bring the knowledge of God down to the understanding of mankind in the clearest and most accessible way possible. This was a challenging task, requiring God to condescend and reveal Himself progressively. But through His Son, He has done all that could be done to achieve this. As Jesus said in Luke 10:22, "No man knows who the Father is, but the Son, and he to whom the Son will reveal him."

Reason 2. Because through His speaking to us by His Son, He has enabled us to attain a level of communion with God—through ordinary means—that is as close as what was achieved through extraordinary means in earlier times. Even though those extraordinary methods of revelation have ceased, we are not without the, "visions and revelations of the Lord," in a proper sense.

This is because the glorious manifestation of God through His Son has granted the saints of the New Testament a more abundant share of the Spirit of God than was ever given before. As Christ said in John 7:38, "He that believeth on me, as the Scripture hath said, out of his belly shall flow rivers of living water." The Evangelist explains, "This spoke he of the Spirit, which they that believe on him should receive, for the Holy Ghost was not yet given; because that Jesus was not yet glorified," (John 7:39). The giving of the Spirit is a direct result of the glory of Christ shining forth among His people, a fruit of God speaking to us by His Son.

The Spirit waited until that light and glory appeared. The Spirit of God, being the Spirit of truth, works according to His nature (John 14:17; John 16:13). When the mystery of the Gospel was fully revealed through Jesus Christ, the time came for the Spirit to be poured out in *greater* measure.

The Spirit had been given before, but not to the same degree. Scripture often describes a new degree of something as if it were entirely new. For instance, Galatians 4:4 says, "God sent forth his Son... to redeem them that were under the law, that we might receive the adoption of sons." Yet adoption was not new to the Old Testament saints, for Paul writes in Romans 9:4 that, "to them pertaineth the adoption." Israel was even called God's "firstborn," (Exodus 4:22; Hosea 11:1). However, the privileges of adoption were not enjoyed to the same degree as they are now, with the Church's maturity in the knowledge of Christ (Galatians 4:1-5).

Even at the resurrection, an even greater degree of adoption is anticipated, as Paul writes in Romans 8:23, "Waiting for the adoption, to wit, the redemption of our body." The glory of what is yet to come far surpasses what was before, just as the present glory exceeds that of the Old Testament era.

Reason 1. The differing glory of the Old Testament and New Testament ministries is explained in 2 Corinthians 3:10, "Even that which was made glorious had no glory in this respect, by reason of the glory which excelleth." Similarly, when the Spirit is given in a new and greater measure, it is spoken of as if it had not been given at all previously.

Under the Old Testament, the Spirit was abundantly given to prophets who were extraordinarily inspired. Now, however, the Spirit is given to all believers, albeit in a different way. This gift belongs to all Christians, though many neglect it. The Apostle speaks of this gift as part of our adoption, "Ye have received the Spirit of adoption, whereby we cry, Abba, Father," (Romans 8:15). Again, "Because ye are sons, God hath sent forth the Spirit of his Son into your hearts," (Galatians 4:6). The Spirit's presence is thus a gift to all believers.

In 1 John 2:20, the Apostle says that believers of all kinds—fathers, young men, and little children—have received the anointing of the Holy One and know all things. Similarly, Paul writes to the Galatians, saying they received the Spirit, "by the hearing of faith," (Galatians 3:2).

The ministers and officers of the Church, who preach the Word, are also servants of the Spirit, not just of the letter (2 Corinthians 3). However, their gifts are like those of other Christians and are subject to error. As Paul writes in 1 Thessalonians 5:19-21: "Quench not the Spirit. Despise not prophesyings. Prove all things; hold fast that which is good." This indicates that even preaching, though essential, can include imperfections. Therefore, ministers are referred to as elders, not because their role is less sacred, but because their gifts differ from others only in degree, not in kind. Ministers are chosen from among believers for their service.

This truth is further demonstrated in how the preaching of the Word by these ministers—whether elders or others authorized by the Church—is described as prophesying. Paul writes, "Despise not prophesyings," (1 Thessalonians 5:20). Similarly, in Romans 12:6 and 1 Corinthians 14, preaching is also referred to as prophecy, and preachers are called prophets. The material they prepare through study and meditation is referred to as a revelation (1 Corinthians 14:29). Paul instructs, "Let the prophets speak two or three, and let the other judge. If anything be revealed to another that sitteth, let the first hold his peace. For ye may all prophesy one by one, that all may learn, and all may be comforted," (1 Corinthians 14:29-31). This shows that what is called prophecy here is ordinary preaching, not extraordinary inspiration.

This is clear for several reasons. First, Paul states that women should not speak in the churches (1 Corinthians 14:34). This prohibition applies to ordinary preaching, as women who were prophetesses under extraordinary inspiration, such as Philip's four daughters (Acts 21:9), could speak under those circumstances. Thyatira was criticized for allowing Jezebel, who called herself a prophetess but was not, to teach (Revelation 2:20).

Second, extraordinary revelation from God would not result in confusion or disorder in the Church. Paul addresses this concern, saying that, "the spirits of the prophets are subject to the prophets," (1 Corinthians 14:32). Extraordinary revelation would not lead to multiple people speaking at once, nor would it require Paul to instruct them on maintaining order.

When Paul says, "If anything be revealed to another that sitteth," this does not necessarily refer to sudden extraordinary revelation. The Greek text does not include the word "by," so the phrase is better understood as referring to someone *prepared to speak*, not someone receiving a spontaneous revelation. This interpretation is supported by Acts 13:14, where Paul and Barnabas, upon entering the synagogue in Antioch, sat down (Greek: ἐκάθισαν), indicating that they placed themselves in a position to speak to the congregation. Without prior discussion, the rulers of the synagogue addressed them, saying, "Men and brethren, if ye have any word of exhortation for the people, say on," (Acts 13:15).

So, in this context, the phrase "sitteth" in 1 Corinthians 14 refers to a preacher prepared and willing to speak, rather than someone passively seated. Paul's instruction is that those speaking should take turns, leaving space for others to share what they have prepared. This underscores that such revelations are the product of meditation and study, not sudden extraordinary inspiration.

In this way, the Apostle speaks of ordinary preaching when referring to prophecy in this context. The preacher is called a prophet, and their studied preparation for preaching is referred to as revelation.

To this I may add what we learn from Revelation 19:10, compared with Acts 2:18 and Revelation 12:17, as discussed in the previous treatise on God's covenant with Abraham (pages 85–87). Under the New Testament, every believer possesses the Spirit of prophecy, even if they are not a preacher in the Church. This is evident from the Angel's words in Revelation 19:10, forbidding John to worship him, "See thou do it not, I am thy fellow servant, and of thy brethren that have the testimony of Jesus; worship God: for the testimony of Jesus is the spirit of prophecy."

The testimony of Jesus refers to the complete revelation of God through Jesus Christ, as previously noted (p. 132), contained in the Scriptures of both the Old and New Testaments. This testimony is so named because Christ is the faithful and true witness chosen by God to confirm the Gospel in the hearts of His people. Christ fulfills this role as the Son, who knows all the Father's thoughts (John 1:18); as a distinct person from the Father, for a witness must be another person (John 8:17–18); and as one who assumed our nature, becoming one of us. Because of this, Jesus says, "Ye believe in God, believe also in me," (John 14:1).

The Angel's statement implies that anyone who possesses this testimony of Jesus—which is the mark and privilege of every believer under the New Testament (Revelation 12:17; 1:9; 6:9)—shares in the Spirit of prophecy and is thus a fellow servant with the Angel who delivered these prophecies to John. This is because whoever has the testimony of Jesus does not merely possess it outwardly in the letter but also inwardly by the Spirit (Galatians 3:2). The New Testament ministry is described as, "the ministration of the Spirit," (2 Corinthians 3:8). Thus, the testimony of Jesus is called the Spirit of prophecy because it cannot exist apart from the Spirit. As Paul says, "No man can say that Jesus is the Lord, but by the Holy Ghost," (1 Corinthians 12:3). This testimony is a living word, abiding in the soul (1 Peter 1:23).

From these passages, it is clear, that, under the New Testament, believers are not without the revelations of God. Through the ordinary use of spiritual gifts, believers enjoy the same communion with God—in visions of His glory and revelations of His love—as was once attained through extraordinary means of revelation.

This provides another reason why extraordinary ways of revelation have ceased. Whatever manifestations of God are now granted to our souls come through the diligent use of ordinary gifts, particularly in the study and search of the Scriptures.

Reason 3. If God had continued to speak to His saints through extraordinary means and infallibly inspired individuals, such as the prophets and apostles, He would have kept His people in a less mature state of faith than is now possible. Continuing such means would imply an advantage but consider the personal presence of Christ in the flesh. Of all extraordinary means, this would have been the greatest, yet Christ Himself said, "It is expedient for you that I go away," (John 16:7). This implies that God intended a better state for the Church through Christ's presence in the Spirit than through His physical presence.

The reason is, 1. Because if God had continued speaking through extraordinary means and infallibly inspired messengers, our faith would have relied more on the authority and personal standing of those messengers and less on the evidence of the truth itself, and consequently less on God. This is precisely what the Apostle sought to avoid in his ministry. As Paul states in 1 Corinthians 2:3–5, "I was with you in weakness, and in fear, and in much trembling. And my speech and my preaching was not with enticing words of man's wisdom, but in demonstration of the Spirit and of power, that your faith should not stand in the wisdom of men, but in the power of God." Paul deliberately avoided building faith upon personal influence, seeking instead to anchor it in the self-evident truth of God's Word. Similarly, in 2 Corinthians 4:2, he says, "By manifestation of the truth commending ourselves to every man's conscience."

Had the earlier methods of revelation remained in place, such as in the days of the prophets or even during the apostolic era, people would have been more inclined to accept truths on trust from apostles and prophets without searching for themselves. This tendency is evident when we first consider human nature. Our inherent corruption leads us to rely on human intermediaries rather than engaging with God directly, as such engagement crucifies the flesh, which resists yielding to God. Second, consider the example of the rise of Antichrist. In the apostolic age, Antichrist began to gain influence, and his power grew as the Church increasingly relied on implicit faith—believing whatever the Church declared without personal examination of the Scriptures.

Now, in our own times, as Antichrist falls and loses power, the reason for his *decline* is clear: believers have turned to the study and search of the Scriptures, grounding their faith *in the truth itself*. This approach strengthens believers and establishes them on a firmer foundation. Truth discovered through personal effort—by comparing Scripture with Scripture—becomes deeply rooted, more impactful, and enduring. This is why the Apostles so often urge believers to test the spirits, prove all things, and hold fast to what is good (1 Thessalonians 5:21). Paul even warns,

"If we, or an angel from heaven, preach any other gospel... let him be accursed," (Galatians 1:8).

2. Because God's design includes the exercise and development of our understanding. The excellence of humanity lies in reason, which God intends to sanctify and use for His glory. While reason in its natural state, corrupted by the fall, is inadequate and must die, it is renewed and sanctified in the new birth. As Paul writes, "That which thou sowest is not quickened, except it die," (1 Corinthians 15:36). In its sanctified state, reason is restored and improved, enabling believers to search the deep things of God without relying on *extraordinary* means.

This maturity is best achieved in the New Testament era when God has spoken through His Son, providing the clearest and most accessible revelation of Himself. If extraordinary revelations had continued, believers would have been prone to laziness, relying on apostolic authority rather than diligently studying and using their God-given faculties. God, however, desires that we serve Him with all our faculties, including our understanding, and therefore removes any means that might hinder our growth in faith and knowledge of His will.

3. Because spiritual growth and strength depend not only on discovering the truth but also on being deeply rooted and grounded in it. Truth gained through personal study and effort becomes a part of the believer, enabling them to draw comfort from it, withstand opposition, and defend their faith. Truth received passively, without effort, is less effective. When such believers face challenges, they

lack the ability to respond and must defer to others for answers. If extraordinary means had continued, this reliance on others would have been even more prevalent, hindering the maturity of Christians.

Objection. You may object that this reasoning seems to suggest that the saints of our time are in a better state or possess a more noble way of knowledge than the believers of the apostolic age, whose practices serve as examples and rules for our actions. This may appear difficult to affirm.

To this I answer. First, the practice of the Apostles and early saints is not a pattern for us because they were in a nobler or better position to understand God's will. Rather, it serves as a testimony to what the Son of God, the Apostle and High Priest of our profession, taught regarding worship and service in all ages. Many aspects of God's Word and will are revealed to us through the common and received practices of the early Church, showing what Christ taught both personally and through His Apostles.

Secondly, in some respects, we are now in a nobler and more edifying way of discovering God's will than they were then. This is because their time was a period of laying foundations, while our time is one of building upon those foundations and growing into greater maturity. As it says in Ephesians 4:12–13, "For the perfecting of the saints... till we all come in the unity of the faith, and of the knowledge of the Son of God, unto a perfect man." While the foundation has strength that the building does not, the building possesses a higher prominence and purpose.

This is also evident in that, when knowledge increases most toward the end, it will grow through diligent study and searching of the Scriptures rather than through extraordinary revelations. Daniel 12:4 says, "At the time of the end many shall run to and fro, and knowledge shall be increased." The phrase "run to and fro" refers to a purposeful searching, as seen in 2 Chronicles 16:9: "The eyes of the Lord run to and fro throughout the earth," meaning that He actively searches for opportunities to show His power. Similarly, in Numbers 11:8, the Israelites went, "about" gathering manna, indicating their diligent effort.

Thirdly, as mentioned before concerning Antichrist, although the same light shone in the Apostolic age, and in some respects more brightly, Antichrist arose and gained influence then. In contrast, in our time, Antichrist is falling and heading toward ultimate ruin. This indicates that the saints of today, in some respects, especially regarding knowledge and edification, are in a superior position to those who lived in the Apostolic era.

Use 2. Learn from this what steps you must take to be built up in the manifestations of God to your soul. Search the Scriptures diligently. Study God's Word with care and seek to understand what He has spoken to us by His Son. This is the treasure house of divine wisdom, the mine in which we must dig for understanding as for silver and search for it as for hidden treasure (Proverbs 2:4). Do not look for extraordinary visions or revelations.

If you pursue such extraordinary means, consider that first your efforts will be wasted, and your expectations will be disappointed. These ways of speaking have ceased since God has spoken to us through His Son.

Secondly, you will expose yourself to the grave danger of delusion. By seeking revelations outside of God's appointed means, you step out of the path of divine protection and leave yourself vulnerable to Satan's deceptions. Proverbs 10:29 says, "The way of the Lord is strength to the upright," and Psalm 91:11 declares, "He shall give his angels charge over thee, to keep thee in all thy ways." However, if you stray from God's path, you have no promise of protection.

For example, in natural matters within the realm of sense and reason, these faculties serve as sufficient guides. Christ Himself told His disciples in Luke 24:39, "Behold my hands and my feet, that it is I myself, handle me, and see; for a spirit hath not flesh and bones, as ye see me have." This demonstrates that in such matters, sense and reason, when rightly used, are sufficient defenses against delusion.

In spiritual matters, however, which go beyond nature, you must remain within the Word of God. The Word is your protection because it is God's creative and powerful Word, fully capable of fulfilling all it declares. But if you operate in natural things without reason and sense, or in spiritual things apart from Scripture, you place yourself on Satan's ground and in his snare. There, he may lead you captive at his will.

As the Apostle warns in 2 Timothy 2:25–26, those who oppose or neglect the truth are, "in the snare of the devil, who are taken captive by him at his will." This is because Satan, as a spirit, can powerfully influence the imagination, producing impressions that *mimic* the work of the Holy Spirit. Without discernment grounded in Scripture, what appears to be a conception by the Holy Ghost may, in reality, be a strong delusion from the Devil.

To this I answer. First, while the desires of the Jews, who sought after the law of righteousness, were good in general, they missed the mark because they did not pursue it by faith but through works, as the Apostle writes: "They have a zeal of God, but not according to knowledge," (Romans 10:2). Their error was rooted in a misplaced focus, which allowed Satan and their own corruption to deceive them, causing them to fail in attaining righteousness (Romans 9:31). Similarly, the disciples, whose hearts were set on earthly glory, failed to understand their true advantage in Christ crucified. This is why Christ rebuked them as, "foolish, and slow of heart to believe all that the prophets have spoken," (Luke 24:25).

In the same way, the advantage of believers today lies in being *led by the Spirit* into all truth, not through immediate revelations of the Spirit alone but by the Spirit taking the things of Christ and showing them to us. If you neglect the study of the Scriptures, seeking extraordinary revelations instead, you depart from your proper work and forfeit the benefits of the present season.

The Spirit will not lead you into truth by such means; rather, it will take the things of Christ and reveal them to you—communion with Christ by faith, pardon of sin, the privilege of adoption, the Father's infinite satisfaction in the obedience of His Son, the healing virtue of Christ's blood, and the life and blessedness found in fellowship with the Father and the Son. These are the truths the Spirit reveals, filling the soul and enabling believers to comprehend, "the breadth, and length, and depth, and height; and to know the love of Christ, which passes knowledge," (Ephesians 3:18–19).

However, the Spirit will not provide immediate revelations apart from Christ and His Word. Satan, by contrast, may produce strong impressions on your spirit without any reference to the things of Christ. If you heed such impressions, you will be diverted from your proper work and lose the true advantage of communion with God. Though your intentions may be good, you will fall short of what you seek. Instead of advancing in faith, you will regress, becoming spiritually impoverished and unstable, like children, "tossed to and fro, and carried about with every wind of doctrine," (Ephesians 4:14). This has always been Satan's strategy—to draw you away from the true work of God, regardless of how fervent or sincere your affections may be.

Use 3. From this, learn how to study and hear the Word profitably. Mistakes can occur both in the object of study and in the manner of engaging with it. The rule derived from this point is that we must study and hear as those who are spoken to by the Son, which involves three key practices.

First, give the most earnest heed to the things spoken. This is the Apostle's exhortation in Hebrews 2:1,

"Therefore we ought to give the more earnest heed to the things which we have heard, lest at any time we should let them slip." Having demonstrated in the previous chapter that God has spoken to us by His Son and that the Son's dignity surpasses that of the angels, the Apostle concludes that careful attention is required. The failure to heed God's Word is the primary reason the Gospel often bears little fruit in the souls of men.

Instead of valuing the great things of God's Law, people treat them as a foreign or insignificant matter (Hosea 8:12). This neglect explains why, despite enjoying abundant means of grace, so little spiritual progress is made. After God sent many messengers, He sent His Son, expecting the fruits of His vineyard. But instead, men conspired to kill the Son to claim the vineyard as their own (Matthew 21:38). Christ has spoken with enough clarity and grace to overcome even the hardest heart, revealing the abundance of His Father's house, the privilege of adoption, the sweetness of pardon, and the glory of eternal life. Yet, casual and careless hearing will not suffice. As God declares, "Hearken diligently unto me, and eat ye that which is good, and let your soul delight itself in fatness," (Isaiah 55:2).

Therefore, stir yourself up whenever you approach this work. Consider who is speaking and what is being said. Recognize that if you disregard His words now, the opportunity will not last long. The time is near when you will stand before His judgment seat and receive from His mouth the sentence of eternal life or death.

Secondly, you must continue in His Word and not be *carried about* by every wind of doctrine, as clouds without water, as the Apostle describes in Jude 12. Christ said, "If ye continue in my word, then are ye my disciples indeed; and ye shall know the truth," (John 8:31-32). Those who waver and drift without stability are not taught by Christ but are influenced by their own corrupt and sinful desires, or they accept doctrines on trust from men and follow the changing tides of the times or the inclinations of their own hearts.

To truly continue in Christ's Word, two things are required: 1. The understanding must be established in the truth. You must, with your own eyes, perceive and apply the truth to your soul as the Word of God.

2. Your practice must align with the Word. A person who hears the Word but does not act upon it is a forgetful hearer, as James says: "But whoso looketh into the perfect law of liberty, and continueth therein, he being not a forgetful hearer, but a doer of the work, this man shall be blessed in his deed," (James 1:25). Like seed sown in the earth, the Word is not preserved unless it grows.

Thirdly, the truth must set you free. Christ said, "Then are ye my disciples indeed; and ye shall know the truth, and the truth shall make you free," (John 8:31-32). He also said, "If the Son therefore shall make you free, ye shall be free indeed," (John 8:36). This freedom includes freedom from the *reigning power of sin*, and the gift of a free spirit in the service of the Lord. It is not sufficient to merely continue in the Word unless it exerts a reformational power over you—

changing your heart, sanctifying it, and bringing your soul into submission to the truth and grace of Christ.

Fourthly, you must labor to receive the Word not in letter only, but also in the Spirit. Paul states, "Received ye the Spirit by the works of the law, or by the hearing of faith?" (Galatians 3:2). And in Ephesians 1:13, he says, "In whom ye also trusted, after that ye heard the word of truth, the gospel of your salvation: in whom also after that ye believed, ye were sealed with that holy Spirit of promise." The Spirit is a unique blessing and effect of Christ's speaking, as previously explained. Therefore, to truly hear as those who are spoken to by the Son, you must seek both the Word and the Spirit.

These are the revelations you should expect and labor for. This is the only way to rise above external forms and superficial practices—not by discarding forms, for that places you outside of them, not above them—but by rightly using them to seek the higher things for which they are intended. As Paul said, "I through the law am dead to the law," (Galatians 2:19). By rightly using the law, he was set free from it. Similarly, by rightly using forms—whether the preaching of the Word or other ordinances—and seeking to partake of the Holy Spirit through them, you rise above the forms in a true and proper sense.

It is entirely true that resting in any form, even the mere letter of the Word itself—understanding it without the Spirit—is low, poor, and unprofitable. However, seeking extraordinary revelations as a remedy for this is to fall into the opposite extreme. To abandon God's ordinances and methods, which He has sanctified as means of enjoying

Him, is to strive for a supposed higher state while *neglecting* the very tools God has provided for growth. This pursuit of extraordinary revelations is just as empty and misguided as resting in the mere letter of the Word.

Such revelations were appropriate only during the infancy of the Church or while foundational truths were being laid, as previously noted. When men seek to rise above ordinances by this means, they instead fall below them, languishing in spiritual poverty. The ordinances of God—when rightly used—bear spiritual fruit. They bring an anointing with fresh oil, a further participation in the Spirit of God. This is illustrated in Psalm 92:10, titled "A Psalm or Song for the Sabbath Day," which expresses the comfort of the Sabbath, and in Psalm 23:5-6, which celebrates the blessings of God's house.

For example, in prayer, Christ assures us that, "your heavenly Father shall give the Holy Spirit to them that ask him," (Luke 11:13). In baptism, "by one Spirit are we all baptized into one body," (1 Corinthians 12:13). In the Lord's Supper, we partake of, "the communion of the body of Christ" and "drink into one Spirit," (1 Corinthians 10:16; 12:13). Similarly, in hearing the Word, "by the hearing of faith," believers receive the Holy Spirit (Galatians 3:2), and by believing, they are, "sealed with the Holy Spirit of promise," (Ephesians 1:13).

This work involves: 1. A powerful impression of the Word upon the soul. The Spirit bears witness to the Word, applying it with life and vigor. This creates and strengthens faith, transforms the heart, and brings the soul into submission to the power of God's truth. Without this work, the Word remains a "dead letter."

2. The image of Christ stamped upon the soul. This impression forms Christ within us, as Paul describes in Galatians 4:19. The Word is called an "incorruptible seed" (1 Peter 1:23) because it produces new birth, transforming us into Christ's likeness. This image consists of conformity to His death and resurrection, resulting in the mortification of sin and a spiritual resurrection to new life (Philippians 3:10; Romans 6:5).

3. The Spirit's witness to our adoption. The Spirit assures the soul of its place in God's family and provides the earnest of our inheritance. This includes communion with the Father, the Son, and the Holy Spirit (1 John 5:6–8; Romans 8:16–17).

Use 3. A third use of this teaching is the refutation of the belief held by some that there are no longer true ministers of Christ who can act as ambassadors of God, speaking in His name and with His authority, because there are none today who preach by an infallible spirit.

This argument states that those who speak in God's name as His ambassadors must proclaim a Word that is wholly, undoubtedly, and purely true. This, they claim, would provide both preachers and hearers with infallible assurance that the message is indeed from God. They argue that the first preaching of the Gospel was done by inspired men who delivered the sincere milk of the Word (1 Peter 2:2), sound doctrine (Titus 1:9), which was, "received not as the word of men, but as it is in truth, the word of God," (1 Thessalonians 2:13).

Since God has not commanded or permitted that what was begun by such a Word should now be continued by a Word lacking absolute infallibility, they assert that those who take on the role of ministering the Word without this infallibility act without divine commission. Such ministers are accused of engaging in will-worship and are therefore not to be considered true ministers of Christ, as all Church administrations must proceed according to His institution and command.

From what has been said in explaining this point, we have a complete and satisfying response to the objection concerning the infallibility of ministers.

First, while it was necessary for God to use individuals with infallible gifts during the foundational period of the Church in the New Testament—namely, Christ, the Apostles, and Evangelists—to establish its doctrines and institutions, it was *never* intended that the Church's ongoing work and growth would rely on such individuals. Instead, the work of God is carried forward by ordinary servants through the diligent use of ordinary gifts, particularly by studying the Scriptures and teaching one another in the Gospel. This ongoing process assumes that even teachers in the Church need to be taught and are susceptible to error, as noted in 1 Thessalonians 5:19-21, where the Apostle links several duties in a practical chain:

"Rejoice evermore."

"Pray without ceasing."

"In everything give thanks."
"Quench not the Spirit."
"Despise not prophesyings."
"Prove all things; hold fast that which is good."

These duties are *interconnected*. For example, the Spirit is quenched when prophecy (*preaching*) is despised, even if it contains some errors or imperfections. To avoid this, believers must test all things and hold to what is good. This principle shows that while the Apostles and Evangelists had infallible gifts to write Scripture, the ordinary elders of churches did not, even in the Apostolic era. For instance:

The "angels" of the seven churches in Revelation 2 and 3 were elders or overseers who were subject to error and required correction.

Paul warned the elders of Ephesus that even among them, some would arise speaking perverse things to draw away disciples (Acts 20:30).

Secondly, the very nature of the Church under the New Testament supports this conclusion. The Church is to be built up, through the use of ordinary gifts, and extraordinary gifts have ceased for the reasons outlined in the third reason of this point. One of God's purposes in speaking to us through His Son was to bring the knowledge of Himself down to our capacity. By searching and studying the Scriptures with ordinary gifts, believers can now grasp the weighty truths of God without relying on infallible or extraordinary gifts.

Thirdly, the office of pastor and teacher within the Church further demonstrates this truth. These roles are described in Scripture as belonging to elders (Greek: *presbuteroi*), who are leaders but not lords over God's people. They serve as examples to the flock, going before them in the same duties expected of the whole Church, including studying and searching the Scriptures.

Pastors and teachers are presumed to possess the same kind of gifts as the rest of the believers, differing only in degree and prominence. They are chosen by the Church from among its members according to qualifications outlined in Scripture (1 Timothy 3; Titus 1). These qualifications *presume* the absence of extraordinary inspiration or infallible gifts. If such individuals were divinely inspired or spoke by an infallible Spirit, they would require direct selection by God, either through immediate divine action, a prophet, or an Apostle. In such cases, God would confirm the selection with miraculous signs, as noted in Hebrews 2:4: "God also bearing them witness, both with signs and wonders, and with divers miracles, and gifts of the Holy Ghost."

This demonstrates that the ongoing ministry of the Church relies on ordinary means, aligned with God's design for the Church's growth and edification through diligent study and faithful teaching.

It is no disadvantage to the Church to be taught by teachers who are themselves subject to error. This is because we are not called to accept anything, merely on trust from our teachers but are commanded to test the spirits and prove all things. As the Apostle Paul warns, "If we, or an angel from heaven, preach any other gospel unto you than that which we have preached unto you, let him be accursed," (Galatians 1:8).

In fact, it is for our benefit that our leaders, who go before us in studying and teaching Scripture, share the same nature and limitations as we do. Their strengths encourage us to diligence and industry in our own study, while their shortcomings remind us of the necessity of personal examination and effort lest we be misled. If God had continued to provide teachers with infallible gifts, it would have discouraged the laborious and diligent study of the Scriptures that is now required of us—a point demonstrated earlier in this discussion.

Question: How then can such fallible individuals speak to the people as ambassadors of God and in His name, ensuring that the people receive the message with confidence in its divine authority and as the Word of God?

Answer: If the people were expected to receive the truth solely based on the credibility of their teachers, then it would indeed require infallible messengers. However, the foundation of our faith is not the personal authority of our teachers, though we are to respect them appropriately. Rather, our faith rests on two much firmer grounds:

1. The self-evidencing nature of truth. The truth of God's Word carries its own light and power, which commends itself to the conscience of believers. Paul exemplifies this when he says, "I speak as to wise men; judge ye what I say," (1 Corinthians 10:15), and again in Galatians

1:8–9: "If we, or an angel from heaven, preach any other gospel unto you than that which we have preached unto you, let him be accursed." Paul's ministry relied not on personal authority but on the manifestation of the truth, as he explains in 2 Corinthians 4:2: "By manifestation of the truth commending ourselves to every man's conscience in the sight of God."

The truth revealed in Scripture concerning God, Christ, and humanity is presented in such harmony and agreement that it exceeds human invention. Each part bears witness to and illuminates the others, forming a body of light that true believers recognize as the Word of God. This is similar to the way light is self-evident to those who see it. Therefore, faith is not dependent solely on the credibility of teachers, no matter how trustworthy, but on the inherent truth and coherence of God's Word.

2. The inward testimony and work of the Holy Spirit. Human reason alone, even when confronted with the self-evidencing nature of truth, is insufficient due to the corruption and blindness of the human heart. Without divine intervention, "seeing they see not, and hearing they hear not, neither do they understand," (Matthew 13:13). In this way, faith ultimately depends on the inward work of God's Spirit, which opens the heart, enables understanding, and produces belief.

Christ promised, "The Holy Ghost... shall teach you all things," (John 14:26) and "guide you into all truth," (John 16:13). John writes, "Ye have an unction from the Holy One, and ye know all things," (1 John 2:20) and, "He which establishes us with you in Christ, and hath anointed us, is God, who hath also sealed us, and given the earnest of the Spirit in our hearts," (2 Corinthians 1:21–22).

This inward teaching of the Spirit was demonstrated even during Christ's ministry. In John 6, when the Jews dismissed Him, saying, "Is not this the carpenter?" Christ explained their unbelief by stating, "No man can come to me, except the Father which hath sent me draw him," (John 6:44). Their rejection arose from *not* being taught of God.

Thus, the authority of God's Word is confirmed not only by its intrinsic truth but also by the Spirit's work in the hearts of believers, ensuring they recognize and receive *it* as the Word of God. This combination allows even fallible teachers to serve as God's ambassadors, as the power of their ministry ultimately rests on God's truth and Spirit, not on their own infallibility.

Question. How does the Spirit accomplish this?

Answer. First, the Spirit does *not* accomplish this through extraordinary or immediate revelations. As shown in John 16:13, "The Spirit shall not speak of himself." The Spirit does not directly declare to any person, "This is truth," or "This is Scripture," or "This is the Word of God."

Secondly, the Spirit accomplishes this instead by sanctifying us through the truth. As Christ prayed, "Sanctify them through thy truth: thy word is truth," (John 17:17). Similarly, Christ declared, "If any man will do his will, he shall know of the doctrine, whether it be of God, or whether I speak of myself," (John 7:17). The Apostle Peter affirms this in 1 Peter 1:23–25, stating that the Word is, "the incorruptible seed" of God because it "liveth and abideth forever." This implies that the Word does not abide where it does not live. It becomes an abiding Word in the soul when it is made a sanctifying Word—when the Spirit accompanies it and serves as a fountain of life in the believer.

In this sanctifying work, the Spirit leads us to believe that the Word is indeed the truth of God. This occurs through three key aspects:

1. Surrender to the power of truth. In sanctification, the Spirit works within a person to surrender themselves fully to the power of God's truth. This surrender occurs in every faculty of their being. Sanctification involves being set apart for God, and in voluntary agents, it requires willingly yielding oneself to God. Without this voluntary surrender, the will is not sanctified, and the individual is not truly set apart for God.

In the sanctification of the understanding, the mind becomes active in its own illumination and submits to the authority and power of God's Word. This process of giving oneself to God's truth produces a belief that the Word is indeed His truth.

2. Deliverance from the corrupt inclinations of the heart. As the Spirit sanctifies, it works to free the believer from the corrupt biases and inclinations of their heart. These biases are the root of darkness and unbelief and the source of the evasions and excuses that keep individuals from acknowledging God's authority in His Word.

As Paul writes, "Men of corrupt minds, reprobate concerning the faith," (2 Timothy 3:8) are those whose corruption blinds them to the truth of God. By sanctification, the Spirit progressively overcomes these corruptions, enabling believers to see and embrace the Word as the truth of God.

Through these means, the Spirit sanctifies believers, making the Word not only a light to their understanding but also an abiding and transformative power in their lives.

Thirdly, in the work of sanctification, the soul experiences the infinite power of God through *His truth*. This power is evident in the mortification of sin, the renewal of the soul in righteousness, and the filling of the soul with comfort. Though this work is often carried on secretly within the soul and may not always be consciously recognized in the moment, the soul that undergoes sanctification silently acknowledges the power of the Word and God's presence within it. This acknowledgment persists even when the corruption of the unregenerate part of the soul raises doubts or attempts to suppress the recognition of this power.

From this, it is clear that our belief in the truth of the Word as the Word of God, rests on more than the credibility of those who teach us. While such teachers may still be acknowledged as ambassadors of Christ, speaking in His name and authority, this acknowledgment is founded on two key considerations:

1. The nature of their work. Teachers instruct us in the truth of God. Though much of the truth may go

unnoticed or not understood due to the weaknesses of both teacher and hearer, their teaching still conveys particular truths. Even if only a small portion of the Gospel's truth is understood and embraced through their instruction, that portion is received as the Word of God.

It is important to recognize that receiving the truth of God does not imply an immediate and complete grasp of all His truth. This is true even if the teaching comes from individuals with infallible gifts, as we can only receive what we understand. Similarly, when we receive even a small portion of truth as truth, we must acknowledge it as coming from God, for He alone is the source of all truth. As Christ prayed, "Sanctify them through thy truth, thy word is truth," (John 17:17).

The truths revealed in the Gospel are such that no one but God could make them known. For this reason, whenever a teacher successfully conveys any truth to our understanding, they are rightly said, by the nature of their work, to speak to us in the name and authority of God.

2. The acknowledgment of God's authority in the truth received. Only what is received as truth can truly be acknowledged as coming in God's authority, whether the teacher possesses infallible gifts or not. Therefore, as long as a teacher is able to bring any aspect of the truth to light for our understanding, they serve as instruments through whom God speaks to us.

In this way, the authority of teachers as ambassadors of Christ rests not on their personal infallibility but on their faithful communication of God's truth, which the Spirit uses to sanctify and transform those who hear and believe.

Secondly, the authority of ministers also arises from the nature of their office. Ministers are consecrated and appointed by God's institution, set apart to represent Christ Himself to the Church. As Christ said, "He that receiveth you receiveth me; and he that despiseth you despiseth me," (Luke 10:16). Paul echoes this in 2 Corinthians 5:20, "We are ambassadors for Christ, as though God did beseech you by us, we pray you in Christ's stead, be ye reconciled to God." This role was not limited to Apostles and Evangelists; it extends to pastors and teachers, whom Christ also gave, "for the work of the ministry," (Ephesians 4:11–12).

Through the word of institution, ministers stand in this capacity not because of personal infallibility or freedom from error, but because the ministry itself is an ordinance of God. The purpose of this ordinance is to reveal God's truth gradually and to communicate that truth to the soul with the same authority and power as if God Himself were speaking directly. God could have spoken directly to His people at all times, but He chose instead to work through human ministers to meet the capacity and condition of His people. As Elihu said to Job, "His terror shall not make me afraid," (Job 33:7). Through this design, the knowledge of God is delivered in ways suitable for human reception, yet it remains truly His Word.

In this arrangement, the ordinances of God serve as means by which He gives Himself to His people. What cannot be received directly is equivalently or effectively made available through His appointed means. This is why Scripture often calls a false ordinance an idol or a false god, for God's ordinances are to represent Him and to function as His instruments to the soul.

For example: in the Lord's Supper, while the bread and wine are not Christ's body and blood in their natural substance, they are, by the ordinance of God, the means of communion with His body and blood. Thus, in effect and equivalence, they serve as Christ's body and blood to us.

Similarly, the Church is called the body and house of Christ. Though the visible Church may include hypocrites and is not in itself Christ's mystical body, it is His ordinance where believers enjoy communion with Him. Thus, in equivalence and effect, the Church is Christ's body and house (1 Corinthians 12:27; Ephesians 2:22).

This principle applies *equally* to ministers. Although they are fallible and subject to error, their function as ministers is *established by Christ*. When they convey truth, it is delivered in the same authority as if Christ Himself had spoken it.

Further clarity: the New Testament ministry is described as, "a ministration of the Spirit," (2 Corinthians 3:8). Not only the Apostles and Evangelists but also pastors and teachers are part of this ministry. As Paul notes, the Galatian churches, who were likely converted not by Apostles but by ordinary ministers, received the Spirit through, "the hearing of faith," (Galatians 3:2).

Thus, through the ministry of these teachers, believers are made partakers of the Holy Ghost, and the

Word, when received fruitfully, is recognized as being taught by God Himself. Consequently, it can rightly be said that believers receive the Word from ministers as if it were spoken by God in His name and stead.

From all this, it becomes evident that even without infallibility, ministers can be true servants of Christ, speaking to the people as His ambassadors.

Use 4: This also corrects the misconception of those who, emphasizing the Spirit's teaching, *dismiss human learning as unnecessary* for ministers of the Gospel. The Spirit of God uses ordinary gifts to accomplish His work. Even unbelievers can be instruments in building up believers, just as those who perished in the flood helped to construct the ark that saved Noah and his family. Christ Himself acknowledged this when He spoke of those who would say, "Lord, Lord, have we not prophesied in thy name?" (Matthew 7:22), indicating that even those outside salvation can serve as tools in God's purposes.

Were we to expect the extraordinary revelations that enabled the Apostles in their work, even then human learning would not be without value. The Spirit of God can make use of all natural advantages, including this. The Apostle Paul, having been brought up at the feet of Gamaliel, employed his learning effectively in his ministry. How much more, now that extraordinary revelations have ceased, does human learning serve a vital role in the Church of God. It expands and sharpens the understanding, equipping individuals to study the Scriptures and instruct others. The Spirit of God has used such learning to overthrow and confound Antichrist, and as the Church is built up through the use of ordinary gifts, it will continue to be an instrument to advance His work toward greater perfection.

In Christ, God has brought down the knowledge of Himself to our capacity. By revealing Himself in the properties and affections of human nature, He has made Himself accessible. Accordingly, the Spirit of Christ works within us in a manner suited to our humanity, as the Spirit of the second Adam (1 Corinthians 15:47). Though His work is powerful, it is also gentle, engaging our participation and making us active in the process. As Christ declared, "He shall guide you into all truth," (John 16:13). The Spirit works progressively, taking time, employing means, and engaging every faculty within us, including reason. By improving reason through human learning, the Spirit brings greater light and understanding, working through this means for His purposes.

While it is true that reason and learning, apart from the Spirit's sanctifying work, amount to a light that is ultimately darkness, when sanctified, they become a great aid to the Spirit's work both in us and through us. Learning, like any good thing, can be misused, and its corruption can produce great harm. However, we should not let the potential for misuse lead us to reject or neglect its rightful use, for this would deprive us of one of God's choicest blessings in the world.

The Scriptures must remain a Christian's chief study. As it is written, "The testimony of the Lord is sure, making wise the simple," (Psalm 19:7). "Blessed is the man that maketh it his delight and meditation," (Psalm 1:2). The goal is to know Christ and Him crucified, to be taught by Him as the truth is in Jesus, and to gain full assurance of understanding the mystery of God, the Father, and Christ, "in whom are hid all the treasures of wisdom and knowledge," (Colossians 2:2–3). Compared to this spiritual and heavenly wisdom, all other learning is of little value. Yet, because this divine wisdom surpasses all, it also elevates the value of other learning, making it useful and subservient to its end. True friends of Scripture-learning cannot reasonably be enemies of human learning, as the latter supports the former.

Let *all* who profess the true religion and cherish the truth be advocates and supporters of such learning.

Light in Darkness

Psalm 65:5: *"By terrible things in righteousness wilt thou answer us, O God of our salvation; who art the confidence of all the ends of the earth, and of them that are afar off upon the sea."*

In the verses preceding my text, we find a declaration of the blessedness enjoyed by God's people as those who dwell in His house. The psalmist proclaims, "Blessed is the man whom thou choosest, and causest to approach unto thee, that he may dwell in thy courts, we shall be satisfied with the goodness of thy house, even of thy holy temple." The blessings that satisfy God's saints are called the, "goodness of His house" because they are granted in response to the prayers and petitions made there. As Christ declared, "Is it not written, My house shall be called of all nations the house of prayer?" (Mark 11:17). God's *people* are His house (Hebrews 3:6), and therefore they are a praying people. For this reason, the psalmist, reflecting on the goodness of God's house, addresses Him as, "O thou that hearest prayer, unto thee shall all flesh come," (Psalm 65:2).

In our text, the psalmist reveals how the Lord answers the desires of His people, presenting this in terms of, 1. The Nature of the Things Obtained. God answers His people, "by terrible things," and "in righteousness," regardless of how dreadful those things may appear.

This involves both justice and desert, as seen in Psalm 99:8: "Thou answered them, O Lord our God, thou was a God that forgave them, though thou took vengeance of their inventions," as well as ultimate gain for His people, for all is done in response to their prayers.

2. The Character of the Giver: He answers as, "the God of their salvation." Even when He declares of His people, "They shall be as the morning cloud, and as the early dew that passes away, as the chaff that is driven with the whirlwind out of the floor, and as the smoke out of the chimney," He still affirms, "Yet I am the Lord thy God from the land of Egypt, and thou shalt know no god but me, for there is no savior beside me," (Hosea 13:3-4).

And He also answers as the God who is, "the confidence of all the ends of the earth, and of them that are afar off upon the sea." However dreadful His answers may seem, His people will *always* have reason to trust Him.

Summarizing these ideas, we may draw two conclusions from the text: 1) The Lord answers the prayers of His people with terrible things, and 2) However dreadful those answers appear, all is done in righteousness. He remains the God of their salvation and the confidence of His saints.

Doctrine: *The Lord Answers His People with Terrible Things.* Just as the heavens respond to the earth with both gentle rains and fierce storms, so the Lord answers His people in ways that may not please them at first. David testifies, "O God, thou art terrible out of thy holy places," (Psalm 68:35). These "holy places" are where God is said to hear His people: "I cried unto the Lord with my voice, and he heard me out of his holy hill," (Psalm 3:4), and again, "In my distress I called upon the Lord... he heard my voice out of his temple," (Psalm 18:6). While comfort comes from these places, so too does terror—not only for His enemies but also for His people.

Moses captured this dual reality in his song, "Who is like unto thee, O Lord, among the gods? Who is like thee, glorious in holiness, fearful in praises, doing wonders?" (Exodus 15:11). One great example of God answering prayer was His deliverance of Israel from Egypt. He declared, "I have heard their cry... and I am come down to deliver them out of the hand of the Egyptians," (Exodus 3:7-8). Yet this deliverance was wrought with *great trials*. Before they were freed, their burdens increased; by the Red Sea, they faced despair, crying out, "Because there were no graves in Egypt, hast thou taken us away to die in the wilderness?" (Exodus 14:11). In reflection of this, Moses declared, "Glorious in holiness, fearful in praises."

God could have brought Israel to the promised land in days, but instead, He led them, "through that great and terrible wilderness, wherein were fiery serpents, and scorpions, and drought," (Deuteronomy 8:15), where many perished. All this was an answer to prayer and ultimately for their good, as Moses affirmed, "He led him about, he instructed him, he kept him as the apple of his eye," (Deuteronomy 32:10).

Another striking example is the coming of Christ in the flesh. Malachi declared: "The Lord, whom ye seek, shall suddenly come to his temple... But who may abide the day of his coming? For he is like a refiner's fire, and like fuller's soap," (Malachi 3:1-2). This day was called, "the great and dreadful day of the Lord," (Malachi 4:5), not because Christ Himself was harsh, but because His coming *demanded a refining process.*

The ultimate instance is Christ Himself, who prayed, "Father, glorify thy Son," (John 17:1). The Father granted this prayer, exalting Him as, "a Prince and a Savior," (Acts 5:31). Yet this glorification came through suffering. "Ought not Christ to have suffered these things, and to enter into his glory?" (Luke 24:26). God answered Christ, "by terrible things," as seen in His anguished cries: "O my Father, if it be possible, let this cup pass from me," and "My God, my God, why hast thou forsaken me?" (Matthew 26:39; 27:46). Psalm 65:5: "By terrible things in righteousness wilt thou answer us, O God of our salvation; who art the confidence of all the ends of the earth, and of them that are afar off upon the sea."

Prayer leads to more prayer; the Lord, in granting one blessing, often calls for further supplication. He delights in being sought after by His people and cherishes the voice of His Church, which He finds sweet. For this reason, He does not quickly resolve all requests but *requires* many fervent prayers and struggles. Consider Jacob, who prayed for a safe return and again prayed as he journeyed back (Genesis 32:9). Yet, even after these prayers, Jacob wrestled with God (Genesis 32:24). Notably, when Jacob finally received the fullest answer, even "conquering God Himself," it came at a cost—his thigh was touched and put out of joint, signifying the strain and sacrifice involved in his *spiritual* victory.

We find a similar truth in Psalm 18, which applies not only to David but to the entire Church. The Apostle Paul cites this psalm in Romans 15:9 to demonstrate that the Gentile Church will also give thanks to God. In Psalm 18:6, David writes: "In my distress I called upon the Lord and cried unto my God, he heard my voice out of his temple." The response is described in vivid, metaphorical terms, the earth shakes, the heavens bow, and smoke and fire emanate from God's presence. Darkness is under His feet, and He makes it His secret place. These expressions reveal the awe and terror of God's actions when answering His people's prayers. Even as He reveals His glory in deliverance, His ways often remain shrouded in mystery.

David's experience highlights this truth. When the wicked prospered, David said, "All the day long have I been plagued, and chastened every morning," (Psalm 73:14). God's answers can be perplexing and painful, as the psalmist admits, "When I thought to know this, it was too painful for me," (Psalm 73:16). The reason is that God's works for His people often involve the crucifixion of the flesh, which is a painful process.

We pray for blessings we consider pleasing, yet our prayers are tainted by the flesh. We often do not fully understand what we ask. As Christ said to the sons of Zebedee, who sought positions of honor in His kingdom: "Ye know not what ye ask," (Matthew 20:22). Though their request had a spirit of faith and love for Christ, it also contained carnal elements. Jesus revealed the true cost of their desire, "Are ye able to drink of the cup that I shall drink of, and to be baptized with the baptism that I am baptized with?" (Matthew 20:22). What they imagined as a pleasing answer was, in reality, a painful process involving suffering and sacrifice.

Similarly, in our days, many prayers and fasts have been offered for the establishment of Christ's kingdom. While God will certainly answer such prayers according to His promises (Psalm 2), the fulfillment may come in ways more spiritual and challenging than we expect. The blessings we seek, such as pardon for sin, are pleasing in themselves but often involve painful experiences. Forgiveness mortifies corruption, breaks the heart, and binds us to holy living—none of which is easy for the flesh to bear.

God grants blessings to His children in such a way that reveals both Himself and His glory. Jacob's wrestling not only resolved his fear of Esau but brought him face-to-face with God. David prayed, and God answered by bowing the heavens and appearing in glory. However, this glory was accompanied by challenges, signified by "darkness under His feet," (Psalm 18:9). These instances show that God's answers often call for faith to trust Him even when His ways remain hidden.

Another reason for God's method of answering prayers with terrible things lies, in the means by which His purposes are accomplished. These means are often difficult and painful. Christ's ascension into glory is the ultimate example. God chose suffering as the path for Christ's exaltation: "It became him, for whom are all things, and by whom are all things, in bringing many sons unto glory, to make the captain of their salvation perfect through *sufferings*," (Hebrews 2:10). This was the wisest and most fitting way for God to accomplish His purposes.

In the same way, God often uses suffering to bring about the blessings we pray for. If we ask for the death of a particular sin, God may allow us to endure great losses—be it the death of a loved one, the ruin of our estate, or the loss of our reputation. These trials may be necessary to strip us of the things that feed our sins or draw our hearts away from Him. As Christ said to the Church in Smyrna: "I know thy tribulation and poverty, (but thou art rich)," (Revelation 2:9). The most significant spiritual growth often comes through suffering. The Apostle Paul affirmed: "For our light affliction, which is but for a moment, worketh for us a far more exceeding and eternal weight of glory," (2 Corinthians 4:17).

Haggai 2:7 declares: "I will shake all nations, and the desire of all nations shall come." While the desire of all nations may be prosperity and peace, the means to achieve these blessings may involve great upheaval and conflict. Even sweet blessings often come through bitter paths.

Thus, the things we ask for, though pleasing in themselves, are often terrible to the flesh in their fulfillment. God's ways of accomplishing His purposes—though always wise and good—can be difficult for us to understand or endure. Yet, in all His dealings, He remains, "the God of our salvation," (Psalm 65:5).

Besides all this, another reason is because, in answering his people, God has more to do than simply granting the thing desired. Suppose the things we beg are sweet, yet what he has besides to do puts him upon answering by terrible things. For *instance*:

1. God may need to make us willing to receive His blessings or to compel those blessings upon us; either of which may cause Him to use means of terror. Christ was prayed for long, but who was able to endure His coming? The blessing of the promised land was sought for generations, but when the blessing came, they refused to enter it and spoke of appointing captains to return to Egypt.

We pray for strength against a sin, yet often we are unwilling for that sin to die because sin is part of our nature, and by instinct we cherish it. We pray for pardon, but the sinful heart is unwilling to embrace the full engagement that pardon demands. His oxen and fatlings are killed, but those invited will not come (Matthew 22:4). And how often would I have gathered you (Christ says), *but ye would not?* (Luke 13:14). What does He do, then? He breaks our hearts, pierces us with His poisoned arrows, and sets His terrors in array against us.

We pray for liberty, deliverance, and reformation, but when these are offered, we *refuse* them. We prefer bondage, despise deliverance, *and resist reform*. One man has this motive, another that, each desiring to preserve old ways. God must then use such means as will make the land sick, purging it of its corruptions. Or if men persist in their own ends, He orchestrates events so that even their stubborn aims still serve His purposes—often turning everything upside down in the process. Sometimes people act rightly because their hearts are turned to God; at other times, they act rightly only because circumstances are turned against them, though they themselves remain unchanged.

Furthermore, since we rarely value what we have not experienced, God does not always wait for us to be willing. Sometimes, as though by force, He bestows blessings upon us, winning our hearts afterward. Then we exclaim, "We could not have imagined that Christ would be so sweet!" If God must force a sinner into Christ or compel a kingdom to be healed, it is no surprise that His ways in doing so are terrible.

2. Beyond granting the thing desired, God must also prepare his people to receive His blessings. Without proper preparation, these blessings might become curses to us or be utterly wasted. A man may pray for comfort, yet he is not ready for it. He may pray for an earthly blessing, but if it were given, it could lead to His downfall. If God's people were completely free from fear of enemies, they might turn on each other with as much ferocity as they had shown against their common adversaries. Bitterness and envy still thrive among us, and where these exist, there is confusion and every evil work, as the Apostle says.

The divisions that hinder our current progress would cause even greater harm if our desires were granted too soon. God, therefore, delays, allowing afflictions to humble us, wear down our sinful inclinations, and prepare us for the mercy He intends to bestow. If we were at peace, both outwardly and among ourselves, God sees that we would grow too attached to the world. By prolonging our troubles, He weans us from worldly desires. You can see this in His delays: a worldly spirit often underlies our distractions. If men were more single-hearted for God and less concerned with worldly ends, the kingdom's work would advance more smoothly. God allows some afflictions to persist precisely because they work to remove these distractions.

Thus, He led Israel to Canaan by way of the wilderness—a long and difficult path—when He could have brought them there in a matter of days. But He chose to humble them, test them, and do them good in the end.

He answers us by terrible things because *in righteousness* He does it. "By terrible things in righteousness wilt thou answer us, O God of our salvation," (Psalm 65:5). Consider David's experience in Psalm 18 (as already mentioned). After recounting how God answered Him in terrible ways, David reflects in verse 20, "The Lord rewarded me according to my righteousness; according to the cleanness of my hands hath he recompensed me." He adds, "With the merciful thou wilt show thyself merciful; with the upright man thou wilt show thyself upright; with the froward thou wilt show thyself froward."

In hearing prayer, God often deals with people according to their dealings with Him. Three ways stand out in which He answers in righteousness by answering with terrible things.

First, in bestowing mercies, He often takes the opportunity to chastise his people for their sins. As it says in Psalm 99:8, "Thou answered them, O Lord our God, thou wast a God that forgave them, though thou took vengeance of their inventions." A soul may plead for the comfort of the Spirit, yet walk carelessly, neglect Christ's service, or be consumed with worldly cares and lusts. God answers that petition, but in doing so, He also teaches a hard lesson. He makes the soul see and feel the sorrow of sin, bringing comfort through bitter trials and afflictions.

What God does in answering prayer is part of Christ's righteous governance as King. "A scepter of righteousness is the scepter of thy kingdom," (Psalm 45:6). While Christ has fully satisfied the Father's justice for His people and presents them spotless, His afflictions are not about fulfilling divine wrath—that was completed on the cross (Colossians 1:20). Rather, they are for their sanctification. Afflictions are tools by which He prepares them for the glorious inheritance He has purchased.

The justice Christ shows in dealing with His people is grounded in love. It is a Father's justice. Consider a father who redeems his son at a price, rescuing him from the law's penalty. That son, while freed from legal justice, remains under the father's corrective discipline. It is in this way with Christ: He delivers us from eternal wrath, *but not to live as we please.* Having been taken out of a state of nature and delivered from the curse, we are brought into His kingdom—a righteous kingdom—where we are governed and, if necessary, corrected under the scepter of our King.

Take this as a caution: you must distinguish between the justice of this kingdom and the justice of a Creator to His creature, and that in two ways.

1. First, in respect of the subject: the justice of this kingdom is the justice of a Father, whereas the justice of a Creator is that of a Judge, free of any such relational engagements. A father's justice is guided by a rule adopted out of love, aimed at benefiting his children through rewards and punishments. If a father were to punish or reward arbitrarily, he would harm both himself and his children. Yet, even within the bounds of justice, a father cannot inflict punishment as a judge might without violating his own love and duty. The eternal pardon stands firm; however, God as a Father exercises a different kind of pardon, one which He may withhold in terms of earthly consequences. Consider Matthew 18:35, where forgiveness is refused in a temporal sense, or the case of Moses at the waters of Meribah, where God denied his entrance into the promised land, saying, "Ye believed me not, to sanctify me in the eyes of the children of Israel," (Numbers 20:12).

2. Second, in respect of the end: the Creator's justice aims solely at glorifying divine righteousness, where no sparing occurs. "He stirreth up all his wrath" and "contends forever with the wicked," showing no reprieve. By contrast, the justice of this kingdom seeks to glorify the King's righteousness, which includes the good of the person being punished. Christ achieves His ends through sparing at times, through lesser afflictions when possible, and through greater trials only when necessary. Yet even in His severest

dealings, it is never to the full measure of sin's desert. As the psalmist writes, "He hath not dealt with us after our sins; nor rewarded us according to our iniquities," (Psalm 103:10).

This understanding sheds light on why God's people often experience harsher chastisements than the wicked. His rods of correction pierce their hearts with afflictions that cannot penetrate the "rotten, unbelieving heart." While wicked men may suffer losses or troubles, they rarely endure the anguish of a wounded spirit or the hiding of God's face. Job cried out under poisoned arrows that "drink up his spirit," as he bore the loss of children, estate, and health. David likewise experienced a heart broken with disquiet, declaring, "There is no soundness in my flesh because of thine anger; neither is there any rest in my bones because of my sin," (Psalm 38:3).

God's severe dealings with His children stem from His righteous answer to their prayers. In His response, He must address their pride, self-love, unbelief, unfruitfulness, worldly affections, and lack of tenderness toward His people. All these matters weigh into His answer, making it a terrible one, yet one that works for their good.

God answers, "in righteousness by terrible things" for several reasons.

1. He assigns to everyone the portion most suited to their need, designed for His glory and their benefit. Some receive more, others less, and some nothing of what they request because He intends a better blessing for them. Often, denying a request proves the sweetest answer in the end. When Joshua and Caleb entered the promised land,

many others fell in the wilderness. Yet God carried those faithful ones into heaven, though not into Canaan. Each received the portion that served their ultimate good.

2. His righteous answers reveal the unsoundness of hypocrites and false friends. Those who are offended or fall away under His terrible dealings are exposed as having rejected His counsel. Christ's refining fire and fuller's soap cause the wicked to stumble, rejecting the Savior and proving themselves "ordained to condemnation." As the prophet asks, "Who shall stand when he appeareth?" (Malachi 3:2). Such answers also preserve the congregation of the righteous, for without this purging, sinners would continue to mix among them and share in blessings intended only for God's true children. Thus, as His people are corrected, a pit is being dug for the wicked (Psalm 94:12-13).

These observations illuminate how God, in His righteousness, answers prayers through terrible things. Though His ways may seem dark and inscrutable, they are always just, holy, and directed toward the good of His people and the ultimate manifestation of His glory.

Application: Let us learn from this the great necessity of having a renewed and spiritual heart, especially for those entrusted with the work of God, so that you may succeed in it. The significant task before you, which will serve as an answer to the prayers of God's people for this kingdom over many generations, has been providentially placed in your hands. Consider carefully what you must do.

This work is ultimately in God's hands more than yours; His answer will coincide with your efforts. Since God will respond to His people with awe-inspiring deeds, it is essential that you be true saints, with the reformational work of God evident in your souls—not merely *almost* Christians, *but entirely so*. Without this, you will encounter obstacles and offenses, and even if you begin well, you may falter and fail, abandoning both your true purpose and ultimate joy. Each person, influenced by their temperament and sinful inclinations, risks turning aside to destructive and harmful paths—both for themselves and for the kingdom.

If this were a matter of another kind, unaffected by the prayers of the saints, a noble and heroic spirit—something even an unregenerate man might possess—could carry you through. However, since this work is deeply tied to the Church of God, you will face the refining fire and purifying soap of God's judgment. Anything that is mere chaff and dross (the best of human excellence, unsanctified, amounts to no more than this) will not endure. Only the integrity and uprightness of a spiritual heart can sustain you without falling.

Regarding the natural gifts of wisdom and reasoning abilities, which some of you may possess in abundance through God's kindness, know that unless these are renewed and sanctified by Christ, they remain ensnared by sin. These gifts, however refined, will mislead even the wisest. Indeed, the stronger your natural reason, the more disastrous your fall will be when sin fully provokes it. In contrast, a spiritual heart presses forward smoothly, regardless of provocations. It is not diverted by selfish aims; it thrives under fiery trials, does not shrink in adversity, and can dwell amid everlasting burnings. This passage from Isaiah 33:14 aptly applies to such a case: "The sinners in Zion are afraid; fearfulness hath surprised the hypocrites. Who among us shall dwell with the devouring fire? Who among us shall dwell with everlasting burnings?" The answer is found in the verses that follow: "He that walketh righteously, and speaketh uprightly; he that despiseth the gain of oppressions, that shaketh his hands from holding of bribes, that stoppeth his ears from hearing of blood, and shutteth his eyes from seeing evil. He shall dwell on high: his place of defence shall be the munitions of rocks: bread shall be given him; his waters shall be sure." This means such a person will find comfort in their condition, no matter how dire it may appear to reason.

Consider the example of Saul. By natural abilities, he was among the most promising individuals. And yet he failed and perished in God's work because he lacked *a holy heart*. Similarly, take Jehu, a man of great zeal, whose corrupt heart and selfish motives destroyed his legacy and robbed him of the satisfaction of the work he had done for God. His actions against Ahab's house, though commanded by God, were ultimately judged as murder and brought down upon his head, as Hosea 1:4 declares: "Thus saith the Lord; I will avenge the blood of Jezreel upon the house of Jehu."

Therefore, beyond all other compelling reasons to repent and turn to God—the beauty and glory of Christ, the joys of a holy life, the sweetness of pardon, the peace of a quiet conscience, and the hope of eternal glory—here lies another reason you cannot ignore. If you desire God's work to prosper through your hands, for your own happiness in it, and for your name to be remembered with blessing by posterity, then do not labor outwardly only in your efforts but also inwardly within your hearts. Believe in Christ and turn fully to God, ensuring that His work within you is complete so that you are not merely professing Christians but *true* Christians indeed.

To those who have already begun, strive to grow further in Christ, deepening into a more spiritual and heavenly disposition. To those who are still strangers to the life of God, now is the time to begin. Do not fear such a work, for while it is true that the God of your salvation will answer you with awe-inspiring deeds, the pardon of sin will break your heart. Know this: when Christ enters your soul, He comes with fire. "He shall baptize you with the Holy Ghost and with fire," and you will face various trials. Yet all will be done in righteousness, and He will remain a God of salvation throughout. You will find no cause to complain against Him, even amid trials. Instead, you will dwell with the consuming fire, meaning you will experience peace, quiet, and rest in all circumstances. Therefore, as daunting as His dealings may seem, He is the confidence of all the ends of the earth and of those far off upon the seas—seas that are most distant from the shore, with their highest waves and fiercest storms.

Ask His people if any have ever had reason to complain. Only those who hide their single talent in a napkin find fault, while those who bring two talents to four or five to ten rejoice in His service. And can anyone imagine escaping the awe-inspiring judgment of the Lord by avoiding His service? If God answers His people with such deeds, how do you suppose He will respond to those who are not His—those who despise His counsel, cast His commandments behind their backs, and refuse to be reformed? "If the righteous scarcely be saved, where shall the ungodly and the sinner appear?" How terrible will be His response to them! "He shall stir up all His wrath against them, laugh at their destruction, and mock when their fear cometh."

Application 2: Let us also learn from this where our comfort and security lies in our work for God. It does not come from avoiding or bypassing the difficulties that inevitably arise but from recognizing that the task before us *is God's work*, and we are acting in alignment *with His will*. Challenges in His work are to be expected, and attempting to avoid one may lead to facing others far worse. Human malice and wrath will grow against you, and the tongues of the wicked, ignited by hell itself, will continually find accusations to hurl, no matter the circumstances. Enemies will multiply and regroup, gaining renewed strength after temporary setbacks. Even friends may prove false, resentful, or contentious. Do not let these things discourage you, for your safety does not rest in being free from such trials—it is futile to expect otherwise. Instead, it lies in conducting yourself with sincerity, integrity, and devotion to God and your country.

If your heart feels burdened during this work, do not attempt to lessen it through sinful compromises or by abandoning the truth. Rather, persevere with humility, righteousness, and faithfulness, trusting that you will prosper because of your adherence to these virtues. Even when falsehood, betrayal, or ingratitude confronts you, your confidence must rest in the assurance that what you do for God is under His protection and that He is far more invested in the outcome than you are.

Understand also that when events do not unfold as you wish, do not be quick to blame others. The difficult and trying circumstances that you face often stem from God's higher purposes, which include His love for His people and His response to their prayers. Do not fixate on second causes or external agents of difficulty, for the ultimate direction and outcome are ordered by God's sovereign hand. As David declared, "I was silent because thou didst it," (Psalm 39:9). Accept this perspective and seek to discern God's purposes rather than grumble over perceived failures or shortcomings of individuals.

Let this also serve as a warning against pride and divisions among yourselves, particularly when God grants success. Great victories over your enemies are no justification for hatred, envy, or strife among brethren. Be wary of this, for the God who answers by awe-inspiring deeds may allow such pride to lead to a greater fall. You must remember that His work is not finished, and His purposes may still include correction for your sins. Reflect on how divisions and bitterness were less prevalent when times were humbler and consider how love and unity have diminished with prosperity.

Without love, even the greatest gifts and abilities are rendered useless, becoming like sounding brass or tinkling cymbals, making noise without purpose. God will not remain silent in the face of such sins. He has forgiven much—debts of ten thousand talents—and spared us from destruction despite our iniquities. Yet if we seize our fellow servants by the throat for far lesser offenses, will God not have something to say about this? Fear provoking the God who answers His saints with awe-inspiring deeds.

You have already been exhorted to work out your salvation with fear and trembling. Let me renew that call, especially as one of the Apostle's main intentions in Philippians 2:12 was to urge believers to pursue the blessings of God in this life without turning against each other. Salvation begins here, as the Church is called heaven on earth. As the psalmist says, "I will clothe her priests with salvation," (Psalm 132:16).

Bitterness and strife are incompatible with true fear and reverence for God. The Apostle reminds us in Hebrews 12:14 to "follow peace with all men, and holiness," noting that bitterness troubles and profanes. Pride and self-confidence are the root of such discord, as they forget that God is the source of every gift and ability. He works in us "both to will and to do of his good pleasure," (Philippians 2:13), and He can withdraw these gifts at any time.

Do not presume that your work for God allows you to despise or judge your fellow servants. True zeal for God must not give way to *bitterness*. False zeal, born of bitterness, will harm the work of God and dishonor His name. Consider this carefully. If we allow deliverance and blessings from God to lead us into sin, we can expect further correction. Without love and holiness, our religion becomes vain, and our spiritual growth stagnates.

He who does not love his brother "abideth in death," (1 John 3:14), and "whosoever hateth his brother is a murderer," (1 John 3:15). No murderer has eternal life abiding in him. Let these truths guide you as you continue the work God has placed before you. *Amen.*

Israel's Peace with God

Judges 20:26-28, *"Then all the children of Israel, and all the people, went up, and came unto the house of God, and wept, and sat there before the LORD, and fasted that day until even, and offered burnt offerings and peace offerings before the LORD. And the children of Israel enquired of the LORD (for the ark of the covenant of God was there in those days, and Phinehas, the son of Eleazar, the son of Aaron, stood before it in those days) saying, 'Shall I yet again go out to battle against the children of Benjamin my brother, or shall I cease?' And the LORD said, 'Go up; for tomorrow I will deliver them into thine hand.'"*

In this passage, we are presented with the history of Israel's war against the tribe of Benjamin, an internal conflict sparked by a heinous crime described in the previous chapter—the atrocity committed against the Levite's concubine. The men of Israel, compelled by a sense of justice, viewed themselves as duty-bound to punish such evil, just as they would have been obligated to act against the two and a half tribes near the Jordan if they had used their altar for idolatrous worship (Joshua 22:17, 20).

Israel's cause was just, and their call to action was affirmed by God, who gave them direction through an oracle (Judges 20:18). Nevertheless, despite the righteousness of their cause and the legitimacy of their call, they suffered two devastating defeats at the hands of the Benjamites, losing nearly forty thousand men in total. This failure illustrates a critical truth: the justice of a cause and a lawful call alone *do not* guarantee success.

The text highlights two key aspects of this narrative: 1. The people's response after their second defeat. They turned to God, as seen in verse 26, where all the children of Israel gathered at the house of God. When the comforts of this world fail, the people of God draw nearer to Him. Their afflictions humbled them and drove them to repentance, prompting them to declare, "Come, let us return unto the Lord our God, for he hath torn, and he will heal us; he hath smitten, and he will bind us up," (Hosea 6:1).

2. Their specific actions to seek reconciliation with God. The Israelites realized that their failure was due to their lack of peace with God. While their cause was right, their own sin and false worship had separated them from divine favor. In response, they took three deliberate steps to make peace with God:

1). They humbled themselves through fasting and weeping. They acknowledged that peace with God requires a broken and contrite heart. "God resists the proud, but gives grace unto the humble," (James 4:6). As God promised in 2 Chronicles 7:14, "If my people humble themselves and pray... I will forgive their sin and heal their land."

2). They sought pardon through burnt offerings. These sacrifices pointed to Christ, who, through His eternal Spirit, offered Himself to purge the conscience from dead works (Hebrews 9:14). By offering burnt offerings, the Israelites sought cleansing and reconciliation.

3). They *renewed their covenant* with God through peace offerings. The peace offering, a thank offering for mercies received or a vow fulfilled, signified their dedication to God. As Proverbs 7:14 states, "I have peace offerings with me; this day have I paid my vows." Such sacrifices, when accompanied by prayer and thanksgiving, lead to the peace of God, which guards the heart and mind (Philippians 4:6-7). This renewal of covenant echoed Nehemiah 9:38, where in great distress, the people made a "sure covenant" and sealed it.

Additionally, the Israelites sought divine counsel before proceeding further. Despite having advanced under God's earlier command, their broken spirits led them to humbly inquire, "Shall I yet again go out to battle against the children of Benjamin my brother, or shall I cease?" (Judges 20:28). Their question reflects a willingness to submit to God's will, even if it meant accepting a painful outcome.

The text also provides significant context for their inquiry. The Ark of the Covenant, representing God's presence, was in Shiloh, and the inquiry was made through Phinehas, the son of Eleazar, the high priest. This highlights the sanctity and seriousness of their appeal to God.

In sum, this passage demonstrates the necessity of humility, repentance, and renewed commitment to God in times of distress. The Israelites' example underscores that peace with God is essential for His favor and that even just causes cannot succeed without His blessing. Their actions serve as a timeless reminder of the importance of seeking

God wholeheartedly in both personal and collective endeavors.

This passage elaborates on the importance of reconciliation with God for achieving success in His work. The text presents the historical backdrop of the Israelites' conflict with the tribe of Benjamin and emphasizes that their eventual success did not depend on their military strength but on their spiritual alignment with God. The author explains this through several observations and theological points.

First, the historical note clarifies that this war occurred before the Ark was taken by the Philistines. This contextual detail underscores that Israel's initial failures were due to unrepented sin and unresolved estrangement from God. Despite a just cause and divine guidance to proceed, their lack of repentance and peace with God hindered their success.

The Israelites' turning point came when they humbled themselves with fasting, weeping, and sacrifices. Their burnt offerings symbolized atonement through Christ's future sacrifice, and their peace offerings reflected covenant renewal and thanksgiving. This transformation of heart led God to respond with a command to battle and a promise of victory, demonstrating that reconciliation with Him is the foundation for success in His work.

The doctrine derived from the narrative is that *God's work prospers best in the hands of those who are at peace with Him.* This point is also proven by examples from Scripture:

1. Joshua, the high priest, is cleansed of filthy garments in a vision, symbolizing the removal of sin (Zechariah 3:3-4). This act of grace enabled him to fulfill his divine calling.

2. Isaiah experienced a similar cleansing, where his lips were touched by a coal from the altar, equipping him for prophetic ministry (Isaiah 6:6-7).

3. David triumphed in his endeavors because he was a man after God's own heart. Conversely, Saul, though outwardly impressive, failed due to his unreconciled state with God.

Reconciliation with God provides courage, wisdom, and a selfless focus necessary for success in His work. The work of God often faces opposition, and only those strengthened by divine peace can persevere. Courage, in particular, is essential, as illustrated by biblical examples such as John the Baptist confronting Herod and Gideon's selective army where the fearful were dismissed (Deuteronomy 20:1, Judges 7:3).

The work of God also *tests* the faithful. Through opposition, God reveals the strength of His people's commitment, showing that their dedication is not swayed by fear, loss, or temptation. This perseverance, rooted in peace with God, distinguishes His followers from the world, ensuring their efforts yield spiritual and eternal fruit.

Let us consider what the pardon of our sins and peace with God accomplish for a person. What does Solomon say? "The wicked flee when no man pursueth: but the righteous are bold as a lion," (Proverbs 28:1). A guilty conscience always creates cowardice. Isaiah also describes this condition: "The sinners in Zion are afraid; fearfulness hath surprised the hypocrites," (Isaiah 33:14). But the righteous enjoy *a distinct privilege* in times of trouble. Our Savior speaks of this in Luke: "And there shall be signs in the sun, and in the moon, and in the stars; and upon the earth distress of nations, with perplexity; the sea and the waves roaring; men's hearts failing them for fear, and for looking after those things which are coming on the earth: for the powers of heaven shall be shaken. And then shall they see the Son of man coming in a cloud with power and great glory. And when these things begin to come to pass, then look up, and lift up your heads; for your redemption draweth nigh," (Luke 21:25-28).

A guilty man, however, must bear two simultaneous burdens: external opposition and internal anguish from the wrath of God upon his soul. These combined are a weight that will crush his spirit. "The spirit of a man will sustain his infirmity; but a wounded spirit who can bear?" (Proverbs 18:14). This explains why the wise man states, "For a just man falleth seven times, and riseth up again: but the wicked shall fall into mischief," (Proverbs 24:16). Whatever opposition a righteous person faces outwardly, his heart remains intact, and his courage is unbroken. However, the wicked man, lacking peace with God, has no foundation to steady his soul. When he falls, he sinks into despair and cannot revive his spirit.

Even heathen philosophers recognized this principle. One observed that a man with a guilty conscience fears himself. Unable to account for his actions to his own soul, how could he face death—the messenger of God, the righteous Judge? Pythagoras advised, *Inprimis reverere teipsum* (Above all, revere yourself). Historical examples affirm this truth. Charles IX of France, after the bloody massacre of Protestants, found himself more tormented by his own conscience than he ever had been by external threats.

This, then, is one reason why the work of God prospers best in the hands of those whose sins are pardoned—because *peace* with God instills *courage* for His cause.

The work of God also demands *wisdom*. The enemies of God are cunning. Sin is deceitful, and Satan is exceedingly subtle. Additionally, understanding God's work is no simple matter. "But the natural man receiveth not the things of the Spirit of God: for they are foolishness unto him: neither can he know them, because they are spiritually discerned," (1 Corinthians 2:14). Furthermore, those who labor in His work will often encounter obstacles; mountains will rise before them, as they did for Zerubbabel. Wisdom is necessary in all these cases.

The work of God is like a ship navigating a stormy sea. Great skill is required to guide it and keep it on course. This is especially true for those called to be *saviors* of a people. Christ, as the wisdom of the Father, was perfectly equipped for His divine mission. Similarly, you, honorable and worthy senators, are called to be saviors of this kingdom. This task requires you to labor on behalf of many who may repay your faithfulness with ingratitude or even reproach. Some will revile you, others will criticize your actions, and yet others will do nothing to help themselves. Yet Christ endured such treatment, and so must you.

Wisdom is required to look beyond present discouragements, discerning how future generations will bless God for you. Consider how these present afflictions, though momentary, work for you a far more exceeding and eternal weight of glory (2 Corinthians 4:17). In the meantime, you must act in a way that neither offends God nor undermines the cause before men. As the Apostle exhorts, "Let patience have her perfect work," (James 1:4). He adds, "If any of you lack wisdom, let him ask of God," (James 1:5). Wisdom is the source of such endurance.

Now reflect on the advantage of wisdom gained through pardon and peace with God. Israel, once reconciled to Him, devised a successful strategy against the Benjamites, employing an ambush to take the city. Before this, they lacked either the courage or prudence—or both—to use such a plan. Solomon's description of the wise man in Proverbs refers to the holy man, while the fool represents the wicked. A guilty conscience confuses the soul and clouds judgment. A wise man knows his purpose in any endeavor, but the wicked stumble in darkness. "But he that hateth his brother is in darkness, and walketh in darkness, and knoweth not whither he goeth, because that darkness hath blinded his eyes," (1 John 2:11).

The work of God also requires someone who aims chiefly *at His glory*. Self-seeking individuals cannot succeed in His work. Those unreconciled to God are driven by self-interest, as illustrated in the parable of the prodigal son. Out of fellowship with his father, the prodigal became a slave to his base desires, represented by the swine he tended to sustain himself. Every man unreconciled to God serves some other master, for no creature can exist independently. Service is intrinsic to creation, and even angels find their purpose in serving God.

However, self-love undermines the work of God. As the prophet Hosea declares, "Israel is an empty vine, he bringeth forth fruit unto himself," (Hosea 10:1). The ends of self-interest and the glory of God rarely align. Only those reconciled to God aim for His glory in all they do. The pardoned man can say, "This God is my God for ever and ever: he will be my guide even unto death," (Psalm 48:14). For him, what he does for God remains his own, as Christ said, "He that loseth his life for my sake shall find it," (Matthew 10:39).

These reasons demonstrate why the work of God prospers best in the hands of those whose sins are pardoned. They possess the courage, wisdom, and devotion required to overcome the challenges posed by Satan and the sinfulness of their own hearts. Those reconciled to God aim not at their own glory but at His, and thus their labor for Him thrives.

The Apostle James exhorts us to let patience have its perfect work, and if we lack wisdom, to ask God for it. "But let patience have her perfect work, that ye may be perfect and entire, wanting nothing. If any of you lack wisdom, let him ask of God, that giveth to all men liberally, and upbraideth not; and it shall be given him," (James 1:4-5).

The prophet Hosea laments, "Israel is an empty vine, he bringeth forth fruit unto himself," (Hosea 10:1). Self-interest undermines God's purposes because human desires often conflict with His will. Those reconciled to God, however, have Him as their portion. For them, to serve God is to serve themselves, for they recognize that true life is found in Him. "He that loseth his life for my sake shall find it," (Matthew 10:39).

This understanding demonstrates why the work of God thrives in the hands of those reconciled to Him. Their courage, wisdom, and devotion enable them to *overcome* opposition and fulfill His purposes.

In this way, I have concluded the reasoning behind this matter and clarified it fully. Now what remains is to exhort you *to act upon it*. The cause in which you are engaged is just, and your call to this engagement is equally clear. Take care not to lack the third necessary thing: the pardon of your sins and peace with God. Consider the point that has been explained. God has placed in your hands a work that is His own, one of the greatest undertaken for His glory in these islands for many centuries. This work involves the safety, peace, and welfare of the kingdom—indeed, of all three kingdoms—and to a significant extent, it impacts every nation where the true religion is professed. This work does not merely concern temporal matters but has consequences that reach into eternity, as it involves the preservation of true religion, the gospel of our salvation, and God Himself. If religion and the gospel are removed, God departs as well. "Now for a long season Israel hath been without the true

God, and without a teaching priest, and without law," (2 Chronicles 15:3).

Do not think it enough that your cause is just, your call clear, and your strength prepared. Do not neglect to make peace with God this day. Take heed to the example of Israel in their conflict with Benjamin. The sad history of their defeat speaks to you as the voice of God did through Joel: "Turn ye even to me with all your heart, and with fasting, and with weeping, and with mourning: and rend your heart, and not your garments, and turn unto the LORD your God: for he is gracious and merciful, slow to anger, and of great kindness, and repenteth him of the evil. Who knoweth if he will return and repent, and leave a blessing behind him; even a meat offering and a drink offering unto the LORD your God?" (Joel 2:12-14).

I say the same to you: if you accomplish the work set before you today, who knows what blessings God may bestow on your efforts? Who knows what ruin He may bring upon your enemies? He will gather your tears in His bottle, and they will do more against the rebels than thousands of cannonballs. On the other hand, if you neglect to make peace with Him, who knows what He may do against you? The thought of this should pierce your hearts.

So much effort, expense, and labor have gone into preparing for this struggle, and rightly so. God will repay your endeavors a thousandfold. Even if your efforts were to fail, they are an acceptable service to God, as we see in Song of Solomon 5. Christ knocked and called to His bride, but when she delayed in opening the door, He withdrew. Yet her delayed efforts to seek Him pleased Him: "I rose up to open to my beloved; and my hands dropped with myrrh, and my fingers with sweet-smelling myrrh, upon the handles of the lock," (Song of Solomon 5:5). If God were to withdraw and frustrate your hopes for a season, it would be just. But your zealous endeavors to welcome Christ into this land will be sweet to Him and to you. Even if England is not saved, you will be glorious in the eyes of the Lord. "My judgment is with the LORD, and my work with my God," (Isaiah 49:4).

Still, this is not enough. You must not leave the most important work undone—*making peace with God*. If you neglect this, it could bring ruin upon all. Consider Israel's situation. God was resolved that the locusts should be purged from the land, just as He determined to punish Benjamin. Had Israel made peace with God at the start, He might have entrusted them to complete the task without delay and without the wrath that later came upon them. Instead, their neglect required God to humble them through defeat so they would fulfill His purposes thoroughly. Likewise, if you make peace with God now, He may allow you to succeed swiftly, sparing much bloodshed. If not, He may be compelled to intervene with heavy judgment to ensure His work is completed.

Reflect on how God often deals with His people according to their conduct on days like these. As He said to Israel in Exodus, "Put off thy ornaments from thee, that I may know what to do unto thee," (Exodus 33:5). It is as though God waits to see how you will *humble* yourselves before He declares His judgment. Who knows but that He waits to see whether you will turn from your sins and make peace with Him?

If you ask what must be done, let Israel's example guide you. They humbled themselves, sought pardon through Christ, and renewed their covenant with God. The first step is humiliation. You must actively abase yourselves before God. "If my people, which are called by my name, shall humble themselves, and pray, and seek my face, and turn from their wicked ways; then will I hear from heaven, and will forgive their sin, and will heal their land," (2 Chronicles 7:14). Therefore, set your hearts to this task. Do not settle for outward forms or superficial repentance. Israel fasted and wept, and you must do the same. "Turn ye even to me with all your heart, and with fasting, and with weeping, and with mourning," (Joel 2:12). Bring all your sins to mind, both in their number and their severity, and let them pierce your hearts like swords. Recall the sins of your youth and your later years. Let them lead you to a place of genuine contrition and brokenness before the Lord.

Consider sin in its various aspects: its root, its fruit, its cure, and the object against whom it is committed. First, let us examine sin in its root, which is our very nature. We brought it with us into the world, as the psalmist declares, "Behold, I was shapen in iniquity; and in sin did my mother conceive me," (Psalm 51:5). If anything can break our hearts, it is the thought of this *original corruption*. David, when humbling himself in his penitential psalm, draws attention to many things to humble his soul—his sin against God, "Against thee, thee only, have I sinned," (Psalm 51:4); his sin against knowledge, that "hidden wisdom" which God had given him. Yet he especially emphasizes his original sin, referring to it with a solemn "Behold."

Likewise, the Apostle Paul laments this deeply, despite enduring great external afflictions: "Of the Jews five times received I forty stripes save one. Thrice was I beaten with rods, once was I stoned," and more (2 Corinthians 11:24–25). Yet, he never mourns as bitterly as when he reflects on the corruption within: "I find then a law, that, when I would do good, evil is present with me. For I delight in the law of God after the inward man: but I see another law in my members, warring against the law of my mind... O wretched man that I am! who shall deliver me from the body of this death?" (Romans 7:21–24).

There is good reason why this thought should *deeply* wound us, for a threefold harm arises from the corruption of our nature. First, it makes us odious and loathsome to God. Just as a toad is despised because of the poison in its nature, so too is the sinner abhorrent to the holy God. Poison in a dog elicits pity because it is a disease, and similarly, sin in God's people stirs His compassion, as the psalmist says, "Like as a father pitieth his children, so the Lord pitieth them that fear him," (Psalm 103:13).

However, where sin is not merely a disease but the very nature of the unregenerate man, no creature, however vile, is as loathsome to God. As the prophet describes, "None eye pitied thee, to do any of these unto thee, to have compassion upon thee; but thou wast cast out in the open field, to the loathing of thy person, in the day that thou wast born," (Ezekiel 16:5). Think upon this deeply and let it humble you: by nature, we are objects of God's abhorrence, a mass of filthiness despised by the righteous Judge of heaven and earth.

Second, because sin is our nature, it works powerfully within us, making us slaves to it. "Sin hath reigned unto death," (Romans 5:21), and it leads us captive, as the apostle says, "I see another law in my members, warring against the law of my mind, and bringing me into captivity to the law of sin which is in my members," (Romans 7:23). Sin works irresistibly in us, as it is natural to our being. The natural courses of things are described in Scripture as laws: the motions of heavenly bodies are called "ordinances of heaven" (Jeremiah 31:35), and the new nature in Christ is described as "the law of God written in the heart" (Jeremiah 31:33) and "the law of the Spirit of life in Christ Jesus" (Romans 8:2).

Just as we cannot forgo eating or drinking, we cannot, by our own nature, *cease* from sinning. Does not this thought *humble* us? What greater indignity exists than *slavery*? No slavery is as vile as that of sin. It forces us into the basest drudgery, always demanding labor while giving nothing in return. "What fruit had ye then in those things whereof ye are now ashamed? for the end of those things is death," (Romans 6:21). Sin imposes an endless and degrading toil, offering only shame and death as its wages. Let these truths weigh heavily on your hearts, that you may be humbled under the mighty hand of God.

Third, despite the misery it brings, sin is not felt as a burden by the natural man. This is because nature is no burden to itself. We marvel at how rational men, knowing that sin destroys both soul and body, can pursue wickedness without remorse. They even commit sins that visibly destroy their lives and estates, without an aching conscience. This is because sin is their nature, and nature feels no weight. This state of insensitivity is one of the greatest miseries. To be in the direst condition and not feel it renders all grace fruitless to the soul. That which caused our Savior to bleed on the cross, to sweat great drops of blood, and to endure agony, cannot draw a tear from us but is despised in our hearts. This is true for us all, as far as sin prevails. Let this truth stir us to humble ourselves before the Lord.

Next, consider sin in its fruit and effects. It cast the angels out of heaven. Once angels of light, they became creatures of everlasting darkness and confusion. For man, sin cast him out of paradise, stripped him of his beauty, and deprived him of reason's proper use, filling his heart with madness. "The wisdom of God is foolishness unto him," (1 Corinthians 2:14). It destroys the tenderness of his heart, extinguishes natural affection, and consumes all good inclinations. Sin leaves man exposed to God's wrath and curse, sinking him to hell. Worst of all, it causes man to despise pardon and trample underfoot the Son of God. Christ lamented, "How often would I have gathered thy children together, as a hen doth gather her brood under her wings, and ye would not!" (Luke 13:34). Shall we continue to nurture this viper in our bosom? Let us reflect on the desolation sin has wrought in the world and let this move our hearts to mourn before God today.

Consider also the cure for sin: the precious blood of Christ. The blood of Abel cried against Cain, but the blood of Christ cries louder against our sins. Such is the vileness of sin that no sacrifice but Christ could pacify God's wrath. No creature in heaven or earth, neither angel nor man, could pay the price of redemption: "None of them can by any means redeem his brother, nor give to God a ransom for him: (For the redemption of their soul is precious)," (Psalm 49:7–8). Was not Christ's holy life sufficient? No, He must die, and it must be a cursed death. Not only His body but also His soul must suffer: "Thou shalt make his soul an offering for sin," (Isaiah 53:10). Even all this was not enough unless the blood of Christ was also the blood of God: "Feed the church of God, which he hath purchased with his own blood," (Acts 20:28). Shall the blood of Christ cost Him so much, and cost us nothing? Let this thought break our hearts, as we consider the love and agony of our Savior.

Finally, consider whom we have offended: Christ, who shed His blood for us; God, in whom we live and move; the One who fills our lives with mercies, pardons iniquity, and delights in mercy. He pleads with us, "Why will ye die?... O Jerusalem, wash thine heart from wickedness, that thou mayest be saved," (Jeremiah 4:14). He weeps over our unbelief and rejoices over our repentance. To His people, He has committed Himself as their Portion, Husband, Friend, and Father. Shall not His love move us to mourn for sin, by which we have grieved Him? If He weeps for us, shall we not weep for ourselves? His Spirit grieves when His people sin. Let us soften our hearts today and turn to Him with humility and repentance.

The second point is our fleeing to Christ for pardon, so let this also be part of today's work. If we are in any measure aware of the misery of sin and the weight of God's eternal wrath, let us stir ourselves to take hold of the mercy He freely offers. Let each of us reason within ourselves as the eunuch did to Philip: "See, here is water; what doth hinder me to be baptized?" (Acts 8:36). Similarly, let us say, "Here is Christ, a Savior, a pardon offered—why should I not believe? Here is a fountain opened for sin and uncleanness—what hinders me from stepping in?" If He had commanded us to do some great thing for eternal life, would we not have done it? How much more now when He says, "Wash, and be clean," and "Believe, and be saved"? Why delay a work of such importance, which may now be done more easily than ever, as every day without repentance adds to the hardness of the heart? Why neglect eternity and cling to fleeting, earthly things when Christ has shed His blood for pardon? Why refuse to claim it? Let us plead with ourselves, overcome our resistance, and run to Christ for mercy and forgiveness.

This is not only spoken to those who are strangers to the life of God but to all believers. The burnt offering was a daily sacrifice, renewed morning and evening. Similarly, it is the task of our daily prayers, morning and evening, to renew our peace with God. Repentance is the ongoing work of every believer, especially on a day of fasting.

Thirdly, give yourselves to God in covenant. This is the peace offering or thank offering He expects today. Present yourselves to Him as a living sacrifice, yielding your members as instruments of righteousness to God. Let your hearts be placed in His hands, allowing Him to work His will upon them. Let Him bring light into your understanding, stir godly affections in your hearts, and complete the work of godly sorrow. Let Him also fill your souls with the strongest consolations of His Spirit. Do not reject His work, even if you have neglected salvation before. Turn to Christ now, entrust your life and soul entirely to His mercy, and say, "If we perish, we perish; but Jesus Christ shall be our stay, and His service our employment. Here we will rest forever. We will be His servants, and He shall be our God."

In these three things—humbling ourselves, fleeing to Christ, and giving ourselves in covenant to God—we see what must be done to make peace with Him. Oh, that the Lord would persuade your hearts to do it! Especially you who have never tasted the sweetness of a pardon: God is about to do great things for this kingdom and even for the world. This is a time of His *bounty*. Seek mercy for your souls while He offers it. Why would any heart refuse? Is it because you doubt His willingness to pardon? He is more ready to embrace you than you are to come to Him. Consider His lament over rejecting and apostate people: "How shall I give thee up, Ephraim? how shall I deliver thee, Israel? how shall

I make thee as Admah? how shall I set thee as Zeboim? mine heart is turned within me, my repentings are kindled together," (Hosea 11:8).

Do you hesitate, yielding to the desperate misgivings of unbelief? While you cry, "How can God accept me?" He cries, "How can I cast off such a soul?" Does He not entreat you to be reconciled? What more could you desire? "Now then we are ambassadors for Christ, as though God did beseech you by us: we pray you in Christ's stead, be ye reconciled to God," (2 Corinthians 5:20).

Do you think there is no joy in God's ways and that His service is an uncomfortable life? Like those in Malachi who said, "It is vain to serve God: and what profit is it that we have kept his ordinance?" (Malachi 3:14). Then consider the Scriptures' testimony to the joy of salvation: "Whom having not seen, ye love; in whom, though now ye see him not, yet believing, ye rejoice with joy unspeakable and full of glory," (1 Peter 1:8). Think of Christ's promises: "Eye hath not seen, nor ear heard, neither have entered into the heart of man, the things which God hath prepared for them that love him," (1 Corinthians 2:9). Would Christ die to deceive His people? No. They know His flesh is meat indeed, and His blood is drink indeed. Ask any of His saints, and they will tell you that the comforts they have in Christ far surpass *all* the world's delights.

It is true, some fall away, but "they went out from us, but they were not of us" (1 John 2:19). Try Him for yourself. "Taste and see that the Lord is good," (Psalm 34:8). You are like the buyer in Proverbs: "It is naught, it is naught, saith the buyer: but when he is gone his way, then he boasteth," (Proverbs 20:14). So, Christ may seem of little value to you now, but once you have made a covenant with Him, you will declare, "His ways are pleasantness, and all his paths are peace," (Proverbs 3:17).

Beloved, do not delay. Begin this work today. The heart will resist—*it always does*. The Apostle Paul confessed, "When I would do good, evil is present with me," (Romans 7:21). But drive the heart forward with holy violence. Do not despair because of your sluggishness or resistance. Make peace with God, and He will give you strength. He will help you overcome sin and cleanse your heart. The strongholds of sin will fall before His mighty power, "casting down imaginations, and every high thing that exalteth itself against the knowledge of God and bringing into captivity every thought to the obedience of Christ," (2 Corinthians 10:5).

He will strengthen your prayers, guide your desires, and perfect the work in you. Even you who are far from God, who live without Him in the world, at least in this day, recognize the things that belong to your peace. Christ is ready to receive you, sweet in His embrace, and faithful in His service. Do not forget your soul. If your love for your country and desire for success in the great work at hand do not move you, let the prospect of eternal salvation compel you. If you neglect this peace with God, what profit will all your other achievements bring? What will it profit a man to gain the whole world and lose his own soul?

And let me add one more thing: either make your peace with God today, or the work you are engaged in will not prosper. Your gathering here will not result in blessing but in harm. Through such fasting and praying, you may lose much of the tenderness of your hearts and set yourselves at an even greater distance from repentance. You heard earlier what God says through His prophet: "The ways of the Lord are right, and the just shall walk in them: but the transgressors shall fall therein," (Hosea 14:9). The righteous will prosper in their prayer, in hearing the Word, and in every duty, but the transgressors will stumble in the same things. May the Lord deliver us from such a judgment. I will not continue this exhortation further—may the Lord persuade your hearts to heed it!

Is it true that the work of God prospers best in the hands of those whose peace is made with Him? Then, having made your peace, take care not to break it *while doing* His work. Ordinarily, the effort you make to be reconciled will reflect in your care to maintain that peace, because having obtained pardon, you will value it more, and your strength and resolution will grow. That is why I said earlier that such people can be trusted by the Lord to carry out His work. Yet because of human frailty, since even the best have both flesh and spirit, let me give you this advice: ensure that whatever you do for God, you do it without offending Him.

This offense may occur in three particular ways:

First, it greatly offends God when you accept things on trust from others, especially in matters of religion, without searching out the truth for yourselves and striving to discern God's will with your own understanding. Jesus said, "And call no man your father upon the earth: for one is your Father, which is in heaven," (Matthew 23:9). This does not mean you are not to honor your parents; Christ refers to matters of faith, where no man should impose his authority upon another. He continues: "Neither be ye called masters: for one is your Master, even Christ," (Matthew 23:10).

His Word must be the foundation of your faith. All believers are equal in matters of faith, with none having authority over another's conscience. Jesus uses three terms to illustrate this point: "Rabbi" (or teacher), "Father," and "Master," rejecting all forms of personal authority based on learning, antiquity, or example. These titles are not inherently unlawful but become so when used to impose doctrines or practices on others. Christ acknowledges the Pharisees' rightful authority when they teach from Moses, saying, "The scribes and the Pharisees sit in Moses' seat: all therefore whatsoever they bid you observe, that observe and do," (Matthew 23:2-3). However, He also warns against granting them undue authority, emphasizing that they should assist faith, not dominate it.

This does not mean we should disregard learned or ancient men. Rather, we should respect their insights, particularly when they differ from our own opinions, as this can encourage us to examine matters more deeply. However, no matter how many learned individuals agree on a point, do not accept it as true merely because they say so. Instead, prove all things for yourself. Use councils and scholars as counselors, not lawgivers. Otherwise, you would be excused if misled, which Christ denies: "If the blind lead the blind, both shall fall into the ditch," (Matthew 15:14). If we merely accept others' views, we deny the reason and judgment God has given us. As Paul says, "But he that is spiritual judges all things," (1 Corinthians 2:15). John also writes, "But ye have an unction from the Holy One, and ye know all things," (1 John 2:20). Even if an apostle or angel from heaven preaches another gospel, we are to reject it: "Let him be accursed," (Galatians 1:8). Believers are commanded to "try the spirits whether they are of God," (1 John 4:1) and to "prove all things; hold fast that which is good," (1 Thessalonians 5:21). If you fail to do this, God has cause to be offended with you. This neglect has done immense harm, serving as the foundation of the Roman Catholic system. Remove their so-called church authority, encourage people to use their reason, and the entire structure of that Babel would collapse, like Samson pulling down the Philistines' temple.

Second, take care not to withhold anything from God to protect yourself. Saving in this case means losing—you lose what you hope to preserve and lose God as well. When God places you in a moment where you can serve Him with your resources or your life, do not shrink back. Do not say, "Father, spare me from this hour." Instead, say as Christ did, "For this cause came I unto this hour," (John 12:27). Declare, "I am here with these abilities, this fitness, and this opportunity to be an instrument for His work, to advance His Gospel and glorify His Name. Father, glorify Thy Name!" Let this be sufficient: that you serve a God so good, wise, powerful, and faithful.

Third, do not do the work of God *negligently* or *partially*, for this greatly provokes Him. Little comfort will come from *half-hearted service*. "Cursed be he that doeth the work of the LORD deceitfully," (Jeremiah 48:10). This warning is not to accuse but to prevent you from shipwrecking the peace and comfort you desire. Remember, God's work will be done, whether by you or another. As Mordecai said to Esther, "For if thou altogether holdest thy peace at this time, then shall there enlargement and deliverance arise to the Jews from another place," (Esther 4:14). Neglecting God's call may cost you dearly.

Consider Caleb's example, "But my servant Caleb, because he had another spirit with him, and hath followed me fully, him will I bring into the land whereinto he went; and his seed shall possess it," (Numbers 14:24). Caleb was rewarded with a double portion for fully following God. Meanwhile, those who neglected God and served Him partially were cut off and did not enter Canaan. If you would receive Caleb's reward in the blessings we hope for, then follow the Lord fully. God has not neglected you—how often has He delivered you and done great things for you and the kingdom?

I close with Paul's exhortation: "Therefore, my beloved brethren, be ye steadfast, unmovable, always abounding in the work of the Lord, forasmuch as ye know that your labor is not in vain in the Lord," (1 Corinthians 15:58).

Other Works Published by Westminster Divines at Puritan Publications

1647 Westminster Confession of Faith 3rd Edition (KJV) Bible

A Biblical Response to Superstition, Will-Worship and the Christmas Holiday by Daniel Cawdrey (1588-1664)

A Devotional on Our Savior's Death and Passion by Charles Herle (1598-1659)

A Discourse on Church Discipline and Reformation by Daniel Cawdrey (1588-1664)

A Glimpse of God's Glory by Thomas Hodges (1600-1672)

A Golden Topaz, or Heart-Jewel, Namely, a Conscience Purified and Pacified by the Blood and Spirit of Christ by Francis Whiddon (d. 1656) 2nd Ed.

A Sermon Against Lukewarmness in Religion by Henry Wilkinson (1566-1647)

A Treatise of the Loves of Christ to His Spouse by Samuel Bolton, D.D. (1606-1654)

A Treatise on Divine Contentment by Simeon Ashe (d. 1662)

A Vindication of the Keys of the Kingdom of Heaven into the Hands of the Right Owners by Daniel Cawdrey (1588-1664)

Armilla Catechetica, or a Chain of Theological Principles by John Arrowsmith (1602-1659)

Attending the Lord's Table by Henry Tozer (1602-1650)

Christ Inviting Sinners to Come to Him for Rest by Jeremiah Burroughs (1599-1646)

Christ the Settlement in Unsettled Times – Jeremiah Whitaker (1599–1654)

Ezra's Covenant Renewal and the Pursuit of a Lasting Reformation by Josiah Shute, (1588-1643)

Family Reformation Promoted, and Other Works by Daniel Cawdrey (1588-1664)

God is Our Refuge and Our Strength by George Gipps (n.d.)

God Paying Every Man His Due – Francis Woodcock (1614-1649)

God With Us, and Other Works by John Strickland (1601-1670)

God, the Best Acquaintance of Christians by Matthew Newcomen (1610–1669)

God's Voice from His Throne of Glory by John Carter (d. 1655)

Gospel Peace, Or Four Useful Discourses by Jeremiah Burroughs (1599-1646)

Gospel Worship, or, The Right Manner of Sanctifying the name of God in General, in Hearing the Word, Receiving the Lord's Supper, and Prayer by Jeremiah Burroughs (1599-1646)

Gradual Reformation Intolerable by C. Matthew McMahon and Anthony Burgess (1600-1663)

Halting Stigmatized by Arthur Sallaway (b. 1606)

How to Serve God in Private and Public Worship by John Jackson (1600-1648)

Independency A Great Schism by Daniel Cawdrey (1588-1664)

Jacob's Seed and David's Delight by Jeremiah Burroughs (1599-1646)

Jesus Christ God's Shepherd by William Strong (d. 1654)

Making Religion One's Business by Herbert Palmer (1601-1647)

Presumptive Regeneration, or, the Baptismal Regeneration of Elect Infants by Cornelius Burgess (1589-1665)

Primitive Baptism and Therein Infant's and Parent's Rights by Matthew Sylvester (1636–1708)

Puritan Meditations by Francis Rous (1579-1659)

Real Thankfulness by Simeon Ashe (d. 1662)

Reasonable Christianity by Henry Hammond (1605-1660)

Reformation and Desolation by Stephen Marshall (1594–1655)

Repentance and Fasting by Peter Du Moulin (1601-1684) and Henry Wilkinson (1566-1647)

Rules for Our Walking With God by Jeremiah Burroughs (1599-1646)

Salvation in a Mystery by John Bond (1612-1676)

Scripture's Self Evidence by Thomas Ford (1598–1674)

Selected Works of Peter Sterry by Peter Sterry (1613–1672)

Sermons From the Halls of Church History: The Writings of A Puritan's Mind Volume 2

Sermons, Prayers, and Pulpit Addresses – Alexander Henderson (1583-1646)

Singing of Psalms the Duty of Christians by Thomas Ford (1598–1674)

Spots of the Godly and of the Wicked by Jeremiah Burroughs (1599-1646)

The All-Seeing Unseen Eye of God and Other Sermons by Matthew Newcomen (1610–1669)

The Art of Divine Meditation by Edmund Calamy (1600-1666)

The Art of Happiness by Francis Rous (1579–1659)

The Bible is the Word of God Alone by Adoniram Byfield, (d. 1660) and C. Matthew McMahon

The Certainty of Heavenly and the Uncertainty of Earthly Treasures by William Strong (d. 1654)

The Christian's Duty Towards Reformation by Thomas Ford (1598-1674)

The Church's Need of Jesus Christ by Thomas Valentine (1586-1665)

The Covenant of Life Opened by Samuel Rutherford (1600-1661)

The Covenant of Works and the Covenant of Grace by Edmund Calamy (1600-1666)

The Covenant-Avenging Sword Brandished by John Arrowsmith (1602-1659)

The Difficulties of and Encouragements to a Reformation by Anthony Burgess (1600-1663) and C. Matthew McMahon

The Doctrine of Man's Future Eternity by John Jackson (1600-1648)

The Efficiency of God's Grace in Bringing Gain-Saying Sinners to Christ by Simeon Ashe (d. 1662)

The Eternity and Certainty of Hell's Torments by William Strong (d. 1654)

The Excellency of Holy Courage in Evil Times by Jeremiah Burroughs (1599-1646)

The Excellent Name of God by Jeremiah Burroughs (1599-1646)

The Fall of Adam and Other Works by John Greene (d. 1660)

The Glorious Name of God the Lord of Hosts by Jeremiah Burroughs (1599-1646)

The Glory and Beauty of God's Portion and Other Sermons by Gaspar Hickes, (d. 1677)

The Godly Man's Ark by Edmund Calamy (1600-1666)

The Growth and Spreading of Heresy by Thomas Hodges (1600-1672)

The Guard of the Tree of Life, a Discourse on the Sacraments by Samuel Bolton (1606-1654)

The Light of Faith and Way of Holiness by Richard Byfield (1598–1664)

The Manifold Wisdom of God Seen in Covenant Theology by George Walker (1581-1651)

The Nature, Danger and Cure of Temptation by Richard Capel (1586–1656)

The Necessity, Dignity and Duty of Gospel Ministers by Thomas Hodges (1600-1672)

The Precious Seeds of Reformation by Humphrey Hardwicke (n.d.)

The Puritans on Exclusive Psalmody – Edited by C. Matthew McMahon

The Puritans on the Providence of God by Edward Corbet, William Pemble and William Gouge

The Rock of Israel and Other Sermons by Edmund Staunton (1600-1671)

The Saint's Communion With God by William Strong, A.M. (d. 1654)

The Saint's Inheritance and the Worldling's Portion by Jeremiah Burroughs (1599-1646)

The Saint's Will Judge the World, and Other Sermons by Daniel Cawdrey (1588-1664)

The Sermons of William Spurstowe (1605-1666)

The Soul's Porter, or a Treatise on the Fear of God by William Price (1597-1646)

The Spiritual Chemyst, or Divine Meditations on Several Subjects by William Spurstowe (1605-1666)

The Sweetness of Divine Meditation by William Bridge (1600-1670)

The Trial of a Christian's Sincere Love to Christ by William Pinke (1599–1629)

The Wells of Salvation Opened by William Spurstowe (1605-1666)

The Worthy Churchman, or the Faithful Minister of Jesus Christ by John Jackson (1600-1648)

The Zealous Christian by Simeon Ashe (d. 1662)

Truth, the Great Business of Our Times by John Maynard (1600-1665)

Zeal for God's House Quickened by Oliver Bowles B.D. (1574-1664?)

Zion's Joy – Jeremiah Burroughs (1599-1646)

www.ingramcontent.com/pod-product-compliance
Lightning Source LLC
Chambersburg PA
CBHW031357230426
43670CB00006B/574